TO RUSSIA, WITH GOD'S LOVE

When the Cold War yielded to the Prince of Peace

Mark Shaner
and
David Miller

Scripture quotations are from
The New International Version of the Bible
© 1973, 1978 and 1984 by International Bible Society.

ISBN 978-0-9916358-5-6

Cover design: Cate Shaner

Printed in the United States of America.

I dedicate this book to my wife, Vickie, who agreed to let me invest our entire family savings in the Kingdom; and to Charlie Smith and Robert Clark, who taught me that life is meant to be given away.

To God be ALL the glory.

A word of appreciation

I want to say a big "thank you!" to Randy Coppess, my former administrative assistant who took many hours meticulously editing this book; to Suetta Clawson, who served my alma mater, Warner University, and is quite accomplished at recognizing things that need correction; to veteran Church of God writer/editor Kathleen Buehler, who suggested key changes; to Margaret Stimeling, who served on staff at First Church of God in Vero Beach, Florida, and never let a typo leave the office; to English language specialist Andrew J. Lamb for a final, careful read-through; and to Kareen Pickett, who took the time to lovingly decipher and transcribe her father's journal.

I am thankful for Ed Nelson, Don Pickett, and Jim Albrecht, men who believed in a young man's vision and saw it through. If you are ever walking through a field and see a turtle on a fencepost, you will know it did not get there by itself!

I owe a debt of gratitude to hundreds of friends who have played a part in this story through their prayers, support and sacrifice. These include members of the South Lake Wales Church of God and the Vero Beach First Church of God, in Florida, and many, many more.

Finally, I am deeply appreciative to the many people you are about to meet in these pages who have enriched this book with recollections, journal entries and personal testimony.

Thank you.

Other books by David Miller

The Lord of Bellavista
The dramatic story of a prison transformed

The Path and the Peacemakers
The triumph over terrorism of the church in Peru

Song of the Andes
The impact of the gospel on the Andean peoples of Bolivia

Available in paperback or Kindle versions on Amazon.com.

Contents

How it all started

Let's be honest. The notion of me taking a group of Florida high school students behind the Iron Curtain and into the heart of the Soviet Union in the waning days of the Cold War was totally absurd.

I would never have done such a crazy thing, had not God opened the door.

If you had told me then that our trip would give birth to an evangelical Christian church in a city that built atomic bombs for the Soviet Union, I would have thought *you* were crazy.

It never would have happened, had not God done it.

The story you are about to read is true. The people and places are real. No names have been changed to protect the innocent. We are all guilty. Guilty of using questionable judgment and pushing the envelope; guilty of rushing in where angels fear to tread.

Our excuse? Hunger. A deep, compelling hunger to know God and to do exactly what He asked of us.

The Russians you will meet here knew about God, mostly by His absence. Having lived for seven decades under enforced atheism, they wanted God back in their country. They believed He was the only One who could pull their nation out of decay and despair and give it a future.

We Americans personally knew plenty about God (but, of course, were about to learn a whole lot more). We simply wanted to do something that He had asked us to do a long time ago: go and make disciples in obedience to Jesus' Great Commission.

So to be honest, it was a crazy thing we did. None of us had a clue about what we were in for. Except, well, You Know Who.

First Contact

Diary, April 19, 1991

After five long months of preparation, praying and asking about God's will in this adventure, we are now on the plane. We should be in Chelyabinsk, Siberia 31 hours from now. I have no idea what we will encounter; the people, the language, the acceptance. So many questions.

Who would have thought that I, from a childhood in a broken home in southeast Missouri, would ever go to Siberia? Growing up, my mom threatened numerous times to send me to Siberia as punishment. Now here I am, choosing to go of my own volition! God is moving us on. I know who holds my hand, and I am sure of His faithfulness.

Six excited high school students--Karis Blunden, Shawn Brown, Greg Campbell, Sara Fasel, Stephanie Muhlenforth, Melanie Newcomer--and I are meeting up with David Stone in the Orlando Airport on our way from Florida to New York. In New York we will meet up with Pat and Everett Grayson, a pharmacist and his wife from High Point, North Carolina, and the Grayson's daughter, Meg.

God has blessed so much. I know He is in this experience. As I stepped out in faith, we watched donations come in from Missouri, Florida, close friends and relatives. God has increased my faith through many people. He became so real! The words from Hebrews 11:1, "Faith is the substance of things hoped for, the evidence of things unseen," ring in my ears.

I sure am going to miss my wife and children for two weeks. I will definitely pray for them daily.

* * *

We were not, by any stretch, the first Christians to come to Russia with the express purpose of telling people about Jesus. In fact, Christianity arrived in Russia many, many centuries before the United States even existed.

Andrew was the disciple who introduced his brother Simon Peter to Jesus. Russians believe that Andrew also introduced Christianity to their homeland. Tradition holds that the apostle preached to communities of Scythians and Greeks living along the northern coast of the Black Sea, perhaps even reaching the future site of the city of Kiev.

Ukraine was undoubtedly Christianity's entry point into Russia. In 869 A.D., Cyril and Methodius finished translating parts of the Bible into the Slavonic language. By the middle of the next century, members of the Kievan nobility had become believing Christians, including the ruler, Princess Olga. In 988, Olga's grandson, Vladimir the Great, made Byzantine Rite Christianity the state religion of the Kievan Rus. Russians mark this date as the birth of the Russian Orthodox Church.

When the Mongols invaded Eastern Europe 300 years later, Kiev lost its political and economic supremacy, and the Orthodox Church moved its headquarters to Moscow. Pious church leaders such as St. Sergius and Epiphanius the Wise inspired Russia to throw off Mongol domination and consolidate itself into a nation. Sergius' followers founded some four hundred monasteries which became focal points for Russia's cultural resurgence and spiritual revival.

Constantinople was the capital of Orthodox Christianity until it fell to Islamic invaders in 1453.

Moscow then replaced Constantinople as the Holy See of The Orthodox Church. The Russian capital came to consider itself the "Third Rome" and undisputed capital of eastern Christendom. Meanwhile Constantinople has become the Turkish city of Istanbul.

Russia remained largely untouched by the Protestant Reformation that transformed the religious and political landscape of Western Europe during the 1500s. During the reign of Peter the Great (1682–1725), the Russian Orthodox Church experienced unprecedented revival and expansion. Missionaries evangelized across Siberia, into Alaska and on to California, which at the time was still a colony of Roman Catholic Spain.

In the mid-19th century, revivals broke out among German Mennonites in Ukraine and Lutherans on the Baltic coast. Vasily Pashkov, a retired army colonel, became a Jesus follower through the influence of Plymouth Brethren evangelists. Pashkov, in turn, became a catalyst in spreading radical New Testament Christianity among the upper classes in St Petersburg.

During the final decades of the Tsarist Empire, a movement of Russian intellectuals sought to revitalize the Christian faith in Russia. Reacting to humanistic ideas that had come to dominate European thought, they followed a non-conformist path known as "God-Seeking." The movement produced the literary giants Leo Tolstoy and Fyodor Dostoevsky, and a volume of essays entitled *Vekhi* (Landmarks). The essays repudiated materialism and atheism, warning that such notions lead inevitably to failure and moral disaster. The book created a sensation.

When World War I broke out in 1914, an estimated 208,000 priests, deacons, monks and nuns were serving the Russian Orthodox Church. Nearly 85,000 houses of worship and more than 1,000 monasteries dotted the landscape.

Three years later, the Bolshevik revolution swept the Tsar from power and stripped the Russian Orthodox

Church of its official status as the state religion. Church leaders saw this as an ominous sign for the future. Bolshevism's supreme commander, Vladimir Lenin had famously disparaged religious faith as "opium for the people . . . sort of spiritual booze in which the slaves of capital (*sic*) drown their human image." Orthodox clergy threw their support behind the anti-revolutionary White Army in the ensuing Civil War. The move heightened Lenin's antipathy toward Christianity and when he had defeated the White Army and consolidated power, he exacted revenge.

The new regime closed down theological seminaries and confiscated thousands of churches and monasteries, either destroying the buildings or converting them to property of the State. Orthodox clergy suffered prison, torture and internment in mental hospitals. Believers who refused to renounce their faith were subjected to "mind control experimentation," a euphemism for psychological torture.

At the same time, the new Soviet government encouraged the growth of Protestant Christianity to counter the powerful influence of the Orthodox Church on Russian society. However, the hypocrisy of this type of political manipulation soon surfaced. When Baptist and Methodist missionaries organized compassionate ministries to feed and house the poor, the government saw them as competitors to its own socialist reforms and clamped down. Laws passed in 1929 declared "the activity of all religious units is confined to the exercise of religion . . . not any economic or cultural work."

Joseph Stalin carried on Lenin's campaign against Christianity, further refining his repressive methods. Communist organizations banned Christians from joining their ranks, which automatically denied them access to university education and professional careers. The Communist youth organization, *Komsomol,* sent its members out to vandalize churches and harass worshippers.

* * *

Diary, April 20

It's Saturday morning, 10:30 a.m., and we just landed at Moscow International Airport, which was very dark and intimidating. Going through customs where no one smiled was a bit overwhelming.

I still cannot believe that I am here. We got through customs, collected our luggage, loaded on a bus and traveled through Moscow to a McDonald's. It serves 35,000 people a day and has at least 150 employees. Russians realized we were not locals and seemed a bit intrigued that we had come from the United States. They asked repeatedly, "What do you think about our country and the Russian people?"

We met Marina Kaldina, a beautiful woman from Chelyabinsk, who's been living in Moscow the past two years and works as an attorney. She will be one of our interpreters and guides. She took us from Moscow International Airport to McDonald's and on to Red Square. We saw the tomb of the Unknown Soldier, Lenin's tomb and other points of interest.

When we boarded the tour bus that would take us around the city, it was like stepping back in time. We could have easily been in the 1950's or 60's in the States. Marina kept saying that Moscow International is perhaps the "biggest and best airport in all of Europe," and this is the "biggest and best hotel" . . . "biggest and best of everything." She had traveled to New York City, she said, and now she knows "their things were not the biggest and the best." She was saying this as a joke, because the Russian people had been told this lie for so long. Very few had traveled outside of Russia and had nothing to compare to their country. So, they just believed whatever they were told.

The city in April was not very clean, a bit overcast, not real appealing to the eye. Lots of people are out walking, not a ton of traffic. Many of the people are bundled up in heavy articles of clothing. Not a lot of smiles. Most faces wear a serious countenance, as if determined to be about serious business.

It's Saturday and wedding parties are everywhere, getting pictures taken and placing flowers near significant monuments around the city, a sort of tradition, I guess, to honor prior sacrifices.

On to the airport to take us to Chelyabinsk. We wait in the small terminal for one hour. A bus takes us to a kind of customs office, then straight to the airplane. We board a plane seating about 200 people. It's packed and our seats are in the back. As we walk the aisle, Russian people observe us closely. We are the first American tour group ever allowed to go to Chelyabinsk. We are making history.

* * *

By the time World War II broke out in 1939, the number of Orthodox Churches in Russia were fewer than 500. The regime had arrested 130,000 priests and put 95,000 of them to death. Victims of persecution became recognized in a special canon of saints known as the "new martyrs and confessors of Russia."

This occurred even as the Soviet Union officially claimed religious tolerance and touted separation of church and state as a guarantee of freedom. In reality, the Communist government viewed the church as a "counter-revolutionary" element and feared the influence it would have if allowed an independent voice. Thus, while publicly espousing freedom of religion, the government assiduously set about to purge Christianity from Soviet society.

After Nazi Germany attacked the Soviet Union in 1941, Joseph Stalin revived the Russian Orthodox Church to intensify patriotic support for the war effort. In September 1943, church leaders met with Stalin and received permission to convene a council. This body elected a new Patriarch of Moscow and reopened theological schools and churches.

Between 1945 and 1959 the church enjoyed official approval. The number of active churches reached 22,000 by the mid-1950s. Then in 1959 Nikita Khrushchev initiated his own campaign against the Christian faith, forcing a new round of church closures. By 1985 fewer than 7,000 Orthodox churches remained. Government officials routinely jailed priests or lay leaders who displeased them, replacing them with docile clergy, many of whom acted as agents of the KGB.

Baptists and other outspoken evangelical Christians, particularly those who persisted in evangelizing their neighbors, also became targets of repression. The KGB reported that it was impossible to recruit informants among these "many religious fanatics," raising ominous red flags. During Khrushchev's 1959 attack on religion, an article published in *Izvestia* stated that, "The Baptists and other evangelical sects mislead people with high-flown words, and try to divert them from industrious life."

Many evangelical leaders and pastors were jailed or sent to work camps during this period. Others capitulated to the pressure and submitted to strict state control, which included designing sermons in harmony with Communist ideology and asking official permission to baptize converts. An evangelical movement known as Unregistered Baptists took form. Despite vigorous efforts on the part of the government to shut it down, the movement flourished as an underground church.

By the time the Russian Orthodox Church celebrated its millennial anniversary in 1988, Russia had reached a pivotal point in its history. New political and social freedoms introduced by Mikhail Gorbachev resulted in the return of many church properties to their rightful owner. Local parishioners took on the job of restoring neglected chapels and monasteries. Many houses of worship were rededicated in the summer of 1988, as part of government-supported celebrations in Moscow and other cities. An implicit ban on religious broadcasting was finally lifted, and for the first time in history, Russians could watch live church services on state-run TV.

* * *

The city where we were headed was one of the best kept secrets of the Soviet Union. Shrouded in mystery and a target of espionage, it would have made a perfect setting for a Cold War spy novel, except that James Bond could never get close to the place. Security was too tight, even for him.

One real-life figure from the Cold War did get close, too close. Former Air Force Captain Gary Powers piloted a high altitude CIA spy plane over Chelyabinsk in 1960 and was promptly shot from the sky. The Soviets unintentionally sacrificed a heroic Russian pilot to stop Powers. Sergey Safronov's MiG fighter jet was accidently hit by a surface-to-air missile intended for Powers' plane. Safronov remained in the cockpit of his disabled aircraft and steered it to a crash landing in a forest to avoid killing civilians in a nearby village. Powers ejected and survived, but was promptly captured, put on trial for espionage and sentenced to 10 years in prison.

Tensions between the United States and the Soviet Union, already tense, escalated sharply. Premier Nikita Khrushchev cancelled an upcoming presidential summit in the Soviet Union with Dwight Eisenhower to protest the spy plane incident. Russian leaders took these extreme measures because they did not want the West to discover what they were up to in Chelyabinsk.

What they were up to was building weapons, lots of weapons. Everything from T-34 tanks to rocket launchers to nuclear warheads. Chelyabinsk was an important scientific-industrial complex dedicated to maintaining the military might of the Soviet Union.

Given its geography, Chelyabinsk was destined to become a military-industrial complex from the get-go. Situated on the European-Asian frontier, it started life as the Fortress of Chelyaba, built to protect local trade routes from Bashkir raiding parties.

With the completion of the Trans-Siberia Railroad in 1896, the small outpost soon evolved into a substantial factory town. Stalin's rapid industrialization programs of the 1930s, followed by the frenetic arms build-up during World War II, transformed it into a major industrial city.

In addition to its importance as a manufacturing center, Chelyabinsk became a prominent feature of the Soviet educational system. Today it is home to more than a dozen universities: Chelyabinsk State Agro-engineering Academy, Chelyabinsk State Pedagogical University, South Ural State University, Chelyabinsk Medical Academy, and so on. Its public school system is top in the nation.

Educational excellence was part and parcel of Chelyabinsk's strategic mission during the Cold War. Schools prepared their best and brightest students to work in the research departments of the top-secret factories that powered Soviet military might. With the possibility of war with the United States on the horizon, three of their 150 public schools offered English instruction.

Well-trained mathematicians, physicists and engineers were especially in demand during the Cold War nuclear arms race. That is how Chelyabinsk became a top-secret location. Joseph Stalin built the

Mayak nuclear complex 50 miles north of the city during WWII and exploded Russia's first atom bomb there in 1945.

For the next 45 years, the Chelyabinsk province and its population of three-and-a-half million people were off-limits to foreign visitors. Even Soviet citizens had to obtain special permission to travel there.

In January 1992, Boris Yeltsin signed a presidential decree lifting the travel embargo and Chelyabinsk emerged from hiding. One result was that Western scientists were allowed in to study the local environment. Their findings were staggering. Chelyabinsk, they declared, was the most polluted spot on earth.

Accidents at the Mayak reactor and radiochemical plant were the reason. The worst disaster occurred in 1957 when a nuclear waste storage tank ruptured. The amount of radioactive material dumped into the Techa River was twice that released in the infamous Chernobyl accident three decades later. Authorities kept the accident secret, but evacuated 10,700 people. Nevertheless, villagers downriver of the Mayak complex would experience serious increases in the incidence of cancer and birth defects. Medical researchers found that half of the villagers of childbearing age were sterile.

The political and economic transformation that swept through Russia in the early 1990s would alter Chelyabinsk forever. The swords of the Cold War were beaten into plowshares for peacetime. The former Soviet Union's largest tank factory re-tooled to produce tractors. The Mayak nuclear armament plant evolved into a recycling facility for nuclear waste. The city's schools, long dedicated to turning out the crack mathematicians, physicists and engineers who invented ever-more potent weapons of war, would set Chelyabinsk's best and brightest students on new and different career paths.

Our team had been invited to Chelyabinsk by the city's finest example of academic excellence, Lyceum #31. Founded in 1961 as School #31, it had recently earned the honorific title "Lyceum" because of the faculty's innovative teaching techniques. Students and teachers were committed to exploratory learning. Eventually Lyceum #31 would gain the rank of third-best preparatory school in all of Russia.

We did not know all this at the time, of course. We only knew that no group of civilians from our country had ever been invited to visit Chelyabinsk before we landed there in April 1991.

We did not come to spy, of course. We did not have the slightest interest in the arms race, strategic weapons or Cold War politics. We just wanted to meet and make friends with some of the best and brightest students in Chelyabinsk.

* * *

Our trip to Chelyabinsk actually originated with events in Shreveport, Louisiana, that occurred several years before. In the spring of 1984, a 17-year-old high school beauty queen, Karlana Stone, was involved in a serious automobile accident and suffered severe injury to her spinal cord. Doctors told the family that Karlana would never walk again.

Her father, United Methodist minister David Stone, refused to accept that answer. Rev. Stone began an intensive search for a medical team somewhere in the world that could treat his daughter's serious injuries.

The answer came in an unexpected way. David Stone had created a television production crew as part of his youth ministry in Shreveport and that attracted national attention. He received an invitation to take his crew to Washington, D.C. to help create a documentary of a meeting between high-ranking American and Russian military officers.

During the filming, Stone become acquainted with a general in the Russian Army who told him about advances Russian surgeons had achieved in treating spinal cord injuries. The Russians' success had resulted from an injury sustained by a performer in the Moscow State Circus. Doctors tried an innovative surgical technique on his damaged spinal cord and put him through specialized therapy. Not only did the man walk again, but he even returned to performing in the circus.

The general helped Stone contact this medical team in Moscow. The Russian physicians agreed to treat Karlana as an act of goodwill. They scheduled her surgery to take place during the Ronald Reagan/Mikhail Gorbachev summit in 1985. Surgeons opened Karlana's spinal cord and scraped away scar tissue so blood could flow again. With subsequent surgeries and physical therapy, Karlana experienced marked improvement in her mobility. Unfortunately, she did not recover the ability to walk unaided.

During the Stones' six-week sojourn in Moscow for Karlana's treatment, her father made contact with an organization called Peace for the Children of the World. Through them, David Stone initiated cultural exchange trips to bring teenagers from the Soviet Union to the United States. One of these exchanges occurred in 1990, with the city of Shreveport hosting a group of students and adults specially selected from all over the Soviet Union.

This is where Marina Kaldina, the lovely woman who met our plane at the International Airport and led our introductory tour to Moscow, entered the story. An attorney who had recently relocated to the capital from Chelyabinsk, she received a call one day in early 1990 from Natasha Nikonova, the Russian director of Peace for the Children of the World.

"Would you happen to know some kids who would like to travel to the United States?" Natasha asked Marina. "I have two destinations over there."

"Of course!" Marina replied. "I am calling Alexander Popov right now."

Popov had been one of Marina's instructors at School #1 in Chelyabinsk. He was the first person that popped into her mind.

"Alexander is sharp; he thinks outside the box," she said. "And he has just become headmaster of Lyceum #31."

A magnet school that attracted highly motivated youth to study English and Science, Lyceum #31 was one of the best schools in all of Russia. Natasha approved the idea. Marina called Popov right away.

"I can give you best gift ever!" she said. "They want to send your daughter to the United States, for free. I am offering you the trip. Two American cities are willing to receive a group of students and you can send Vica to the destination of your choice."

"Vica," short for "Victoria," was the name of Alexander's teenage daughter. The destination of choice turned out to be Shreveport, Louisiana.

During Vica's stay in Shreveport that summer, David Stone told the Russian students that if someone from their home city would extend an invitation to a similar group of American young people, that he would organize student exchange in their city. As soon as Vica returned home, she told her father, Alexander Popov, that he should invite David Stone to bring a delegation to Chelyabinsk. Vica knew her dad to be an out-of-the-box thinker. The two men shared a calling to educate youth and an interest in teaching the children of Russia and the children of the United States to become friends. Upon hearing Vica's request, Alexander Popov extended an invitation to David Stone to bring a delegation of American students to Chelyabinsk.

"I can host whomever or whatever you bring," he said.

This is where this 28-year-old youth pastor from Lake Wales, Florida enters the story. I had developed a passion for missions during my college years at Warner Southern College (now Warner University) in Lake Wales. Charles Smith and Robert Clark, two professors who taught mission courses at Warner during the early 1980s, were creating a simulated third-world village to equip missionaries to cope with the demands of cross-cultural living. The village was dubbed Hunger Education and Resource Training (H.E.A.R.T.) and the Profs assigned us students to help build it as part of our own education in missions. The H.E.A.R.T. project got me hooked.

I took my first short-term mission trip to Panama in March of 1981, later led young people on several mission trips to Jamaica and Haiti, and staged an annual stay-at-home work camp in Lake Wales. I was committed to rising early each morning and spending a full hour in prayer, seeking the heart of God and asking Him to use me in ways beyond my ability. I practiced the discipline of fasting with the intention of uniting my heart with Christ and doing whatever God gave me the opportunity to do.

On Thanksgiving weekend 1990, the Church of God in the state of Florida hosted their annual State Youth Convention at the Saddlebrook Resort in Tampa Bay. David Stone was invited to lead worship for this convention. Don Pickett, the convention organizer, invited me to ride along to pick up Stone at the Tampa airport.

As we were driving back to the convention venue, David Stone asked Don about his heart, if it was "in good condition." That seemed like an interesting conversation starter to me.

Don said, "Yes, I think it's all right." Stone followed this with, "Well then, I would like you to go to the Soviet Union with me."

"We are planning to take a delegation of young people to the city of Chelyabinsk next April," Stone said. "Would you be interested in coming along?"

As I listened to this conversation from the back seat of the car, my missions' heart began to beat faster and faster. I was eager to be a part of this venture.

"I'll go!" I blurted out. In an instant, I was intent on making this idea a reality.

Pickett and Stone looked at me and smiled benignly. I suspect David was thinking, "He's too young and inexperienced for this." Don was probably thinking, "This is a dicey prospect. I'm not sure we could pull it off--or if we should even try. The risks are so great . . ."

I would not let it rest. I started giving my ideas on how we could make this happen. I could stand up on Saturday night of the youth convention and ask if anyone would be interested in going. My enthusiasm percolated through the car.

"Okay, let's think about it," Pickett said, setting aside his misgivings. "It can't hurt to ask."

Don and I discussed more details of the project with David Stone, and it was agreed that I would make the proposal to the convention delegates following David's testimony of his daughter's tragic accident, her remarkable treatment at the hands of Russian doctors, and the door that had so miraculously opened for Christian youth to visit the USSR.

I took the stage on that Saturday night before 900 young people and youth leaders to extend the invitation. It went something like this:

"Any students here who are totally committed to Jesus Christ, who would like to go to the Soviet Union in April on a cultural exchange trip, and who would be committed to living out their faith before Russian students, come and see me after this service to get an application."

I thought I would be mobbed by eager students. I anticipated that hundreds of people present that night would clamor onstage to volunteer for this trip of a lifetime. We would likely have to use a stringent application process to weed out the just-average candidates and take only the cream of the crop.

It didn't exactly happen that way.

* * *

Only two students made their way to the stage that night to talk to me. They were not necessarily the type of swashbuckling thrill-seekers that I thought would be interested in such an adventure.

It did take real courage for 14-year-old Karis Blunden to come forward. A budding sociologist at heart, Karis loved studying culture and was interested in traveling abroad as a foreign exchange student. Admittedly, she was thinking more like England, somewhere "safe" where she knew the language. She had never been out of the country, or even flown on an airplane.

Karis had come to the State Youth Convention that year with her parents, who directed the Junior High youth group at their home church in Bradenton. She was very moved by David Stone's story of his daughter and all that had happened inside the USSR. When we announced the trip, she wanted to come up and talk to me, but understandably did not have the nerve to do so on her own.

To her surprise, Karis's dad turned to her and asked if she was interested in going to Russia. Understand that neither of her parents had ever been outside the United States either! Karis right away said that she was, indeed, interested, so the entire family made their way to the front of the auditorium. It was the first time I had met the Blundens. After our conversation, Karis took the next step toward going on the trip, and then the next, until one day it was actually time to go. She would not meet any of the other team members until the week before we left. She did, indeed, show remarkable courage for a shy 14-year-old.

Karis would learn after the fact that her parents did have second thoughts, largely because the Gulf War had broken out by the time the team was ready to go. Mrs. Blunden was particularly concerned about the team's safety, but never tried to discourage Karis from going.

One day Mrs. Blunden confessed another source of her anxiety to her husband. "I'm afraid if we let her go, she'll end up becoming a missionary and never come back to us!"

Mr. Blunden reflected on this for a moment before responding, "Well, haven't we been raising her for the past 14 years to give her life to God?"

Karis's mother conceded that they seemed to have reached that goal in ways she had not anticipated.

Sara Fasel was also present at the 1990 Florida State Youth Convention and heard David Stone speak about the USSR. Terry and Linda Fasel worked in the youth ministry at their church and had come to the convention with their daughter, so all three heard my invitation to travel to Siberia.

"Immediately after the service I sought out my parents," Sara said. "As if my desire were understood without speaking, we decided that I would apply for the trip."

For Sara, the adventure began almost immediately.

"Each bit of information I received during the application and preparation process was like gold to me," she said. "This was before the electronic age, so information came by letter and phone. We were warned that during our two-week trip we would have no opportunity to call home. That was a slight concern.

"The most exciting piece of information I received was the packing list. I remember packing carefully; my parents allowed me to spread every item out on the living room floor. I felt so responsible with my choices, including a roll of toilet paper with the core removed, 'give-away items' which felt so chintzy, and stacks of dollar bills to purchase items on the black market.

"Since we were going to Siberia in April, we were advised that parkas would be provided. I imagined snow-covered tundra!"

Thankfully the parkas proved to be unnecessary because by the time we Floridians arrived, Siberia was in the midst of the spring thaw.

Melanie Newcomer couldn't remember when and how she first heard about the trip to Chelyabinsk. Nevertheless, something pulled her towards the unknown. A missionary kid who had recently returned from living in Guatemala with her parents, Melanie's heart beat for the world beyond her doorstep.

Though only 16, she had experienced relationships across the boundaries of culture, so it was not as intimidating for her as for many American teenagers to go jetting off to the other side of the world. "I'm thrilled with the incredible blessing of being able to go to a place I have only heard of, but never dreamed I would get to visit," she told friends.

On the other hand, Melanie's parents knew a whole lot more about what a trip to the USSR implied. The Newcomers had personal reservations about the project, but their confidence in God and the trip leaders overcame those doubts. They lent their full support to Melanie, declaring, "As long as she is with Mark Shaner, we would let her go to the moon."

I had known 14-year-old Greg Campbell since his kindergarten days. I handled the after-school care program at South Lake Wales Day School and Greg was one of my charges. That was before Greg's mom Rachel remarried. Mrs. Campbell enjoyed just a few short years with her new husband Morgan before he passed away. Before he died, Morgan Campbell legally adopted Greg as his son.

I presided at Morgan's funeral. Greg was only nine years old at the time. Sometime after this, he committed his life to Jesus and I baptized him in a Sunday service at South Lake Wales.

Years later, Greg told me that he chose me as a role model. He joined our church youth group when he entered Junior High, so we hung out together a lot during his teen years. When I announced my intention of forming the Russia group, Greg was in. He had three basic motivations. One was the chance to observe, up-close and personal, our long-time national rival. Another was his desire to bring the gospel to the Russian people. The third: a strong urge to be a part of something wild and crazy in the company of a close friend and role model.

Greg's mom experienced genuine misgivings about his participation, and rightfully so. After all, Rachel Campbell was a widow about to send her only child away to a hostile country. I can imagine that questions like, "What in the world am I thinking?!" crossed her mind several times. Mrs. Campbell could have said "no" to Greg going to Chelyabinsk, and all of us would have understood and accepted it. But she didn't. She knew how much it meant to Greg and she trusted me to bring him back alive. Her parental consent was yet another of the many steps of faith that made the enterprise possible.

* * *

Diary, April 20
I sit on the plane next to two Russian ladies and cannot communicate a thing, except learning how to pronounce "Chelyabinsk" and asking if it is cold there. Two-and-a-half hours later we land at the airport and

are greeted by a welcoming party from Lyceum #31: the headmaster, four teachers, four students and four KGB agents (for our safety).

We are received very warmly, our hosts welcoming us as if they had looked forward to our arrival for a long time. It seemed like a large delegation there to greet us, including the Mayor of the City, Vichaslov Mikialovich Tarasov, and Vadim Kespikov, Mayor of Education.

There are also television cameras documenting the arrival of this historic delegation. The airport is small and more welcoming than Moscow's, even though quite empty. Ours is the only arriving flight it seems, and I did not notice any going out. The fact that KGB agents are traveling with us is unsettling to some of the students. I am perfectly okay with it though and look forward to trying to get beyond their rough exterior. (They played their role well, but lightened up as the week went on. . . .)

We make introductions and proceed indoors. Time is 11:00 p.m. Temperature in the 40's, kind of nippy for Floridians. I met two 11th graders, Jeck and Kirrill, very friendly. Drank some mineral water, and boarded the bus for a two-hour ride to the camp on the lake where we will stay.

On the bus we sang songs like "She'll Be Comin' 'Round the Mountain," "I Believe in Music," "Country Roads" and "Amazing Grace." David Stone was the life of the party. He took out his guitar on the bus ride and led some of the singing. We also sang some Russian songs that David had picked up from other cross-cultural experiences.

The headmaster, Alexander Popov, presented me with a beautiful Russian pocket watch with the Daughter of Victory symbol on it, and gave one to the other three leaders, as well. I was deeply touched.

Then, in order to enjoy Chelyabinsk, they presented each of the 11 of us 100 Rubles. That's 1,100 Rubles. The average salary here is 300 Rubles a month. They gave us almost four months wages! What a sacrifice. Our students were deeply touched.

Our ride took us deep into the woods. We were informed of wildlife such as squirrels, bears, wildcats, deer, wolves and snakes. I hope to see a bear!

We arrive at the center at 12:00 a.m. and are given a tremendous welcome by about 20 adults and students. A history teacher stands on the front steps of the "rest home" - their term for a summer vacation spot, not what Americans think of as rest homes - holding a large round loaf of warm homemade bread with a hole in the middle. The hole has a small metal container of salt. We each tear off a piece of the delicious warm bread, which tastes like soft pretzel, and dip it in the salt. After not eating for nine hours, it tastes very, very good! We found out later that this is Russian tradition. The bread symbolizes life and the salt is the spice of life. It represents wishes for a good life!

Our hosts showed us to our rooms on the fifth floor of the retreat center. I have a room to myself, nothing too large, but nice.

We went to the dining hall at 12:35 a.m. to eat supper. Cranberries, cucumbers, fish, veal, fried potatoes, mixed juice and bread. We sit with our new Russian friends and already feel the warmth from these people.

We are the first American tour group ever allowed into this closed industrial city. It took a lot of work to gain permission for our entrance. They told us on arrival that 100 factories greet us. We will attend English/Russian lessons at school. Lyceum #31 is specifically designed for English and Mathematics students. I feel very welcomed, something like a celebrity.

Back at the dorm rooms, our students were already deep into conversation with their Russian counterparts! The adults moved into another room where a small table was set with fine caviar, sturgeon on bread, *Kojak*

(Russian vodka) and the much talked-about Russian chocolate. They pop the top off of three bottles of champagne, pour up, and begin making toasts. Another Russian tradition.

They toast the opening of our hearts and our lives. They toast to the joy of receiving the first American tour group allowed into their city. Chelyabinsk being a military city, residents were always distrustful that a group of Americans might come and search out their defense secrets. We are pleased to be able to get past these preconceived notions.

Each of our Russian hosts then shared through interpreters about his or her life and interests. They said they have been preparing for our arrival for one year!

At 2:30 a.m. we climb into our beds. I'm simply amazed at the warmth and hospitality. We laughed together and enjoyed one another's company.

Today we laugh. When we depart, we will cry.

* * *

My initial euphoria that Saturday night at the youth convention melted away when I realized how few students were actually interested in going to Russia. But on the way home from Tampa, my spirits took another downturn when I realized I had publicly committed to this venture without following an essential piece of protocol: getting permission from my boss and senior pastor of South Lake Wales Church of God, Ed Nelson.

I rehearsed my appeal carefully before approaching Ed. Yes, I would need time off for the trip, but I'm sure my wife and other volunteers would step up and cover for me. Money? Okay, we are going to have to raise thousands of dollars, but we won't take a dime from the church treasury. If the funds don't come in, we will scrap the whole idea. I know a trip to Siberia sounds risky--plane crash, traffic accident, pneumonia, attack by bears, arrested as spies or held hostage, who knows--but we will have parents sign a waiver releasing South Lake Wales Church of God and its employees--except for me, of course--from any and all liability.

Ed was preparing his Sunday sermon when I walked into his office and asked to talk. He stopped what he was doing and listened, somewhat impassively it seemed, as I laid out the program. I finished my carefully constructed presentation and paused, expecting to field a host of questions, hypotheticals and contingencies. I need not have bothered.

Ed tapped his pencil on the desk a second or two and said, "Okay, Mark, if you really think God is in this, go for it."

What a man of faith! I left his office with greater than ever respect for Ed Nelson and his bold leadership. If I had been able to read Ed's thoughts at the time, I might have come to another conclusion.

"Basically, I said yes to your idea because over the years, youth pastors had pitched similar schemes to me that never got off the ground," Ed told me later. "I was busy with other, higher priorities. I figured, I give you the green light, you try this, it doesn't go anywhere, and then you can get on with the business of reaching young people in Florida for Christ."

Had Ed taken the time to think things through, he might have mulled over the idea a little longer before giving me the green light. Maybe, for example, he would have thought back a year or so earlier to the California bus incident. I heard of a bus that was available and decided we needed it for the youth group. I found out that a member of South Lake Wales church, Dan McCraw, was making a trip to California. I asked Dan if he would consider driving a bus 3,000 miles home to Lake Wales, and he agreed.

Afterward I told Ed about the plan. "I've got a bus coming from California!"

He said "What? What are you talking about?"

"Yeah, we got this bus, and Dan McCraw is bringing it from California."

"This is probably not the way to handle this thing," Ed said tactfully. "We probably should have gone to the church council, built it into the budget. You know, proper channels and all that."

But it was too late by then, of course. The bus deal was already happening. I supposed that was my role as a youth pastor to make things happen.

I often used the phrase in my early years of ministry that it is easier to ask for forgiveness than it is to ask for permission. I probably used this tactic more often than I should have, but I didn't use it this time. I knew this opportunity to take teenagers to the USSR was a venture way too big and risky.

Ed returned to his sermon prep after I left his office and didn't give Russia another thought for several weeks. If he had been able to see the future, he probably would have wondered if he had made the right decision. Granting me permission for the Russian exchange trip would one day take Ed Nelson himself away from his family and church in balmy Lake Wales and into the dark winter of Siberia.

* * *

By the end of December 1990, six Florida students had joined the team preparing to go to Russia. They were Karis Blunden, Shawn Brown, Greg Campbell, Sara Fasel, Stephanie Muhlenforth and Melanie Newcomer. By the second week of January 1991, we had all chosen one day each week to fast and pray. We committed to that plan for the next three and a half months, asking God to use us during the 15-day trip to Chelyabinsk.

We also prayed that each of us would have in hand the estimated $3,000 per person it would cost to make the 15-day trip to Chelyabinsk.

Melanie Newcomer's parents were no strangers to missions. They understood, better than most, the resources it takes to travel and work overseas. Mary Jane Newcomer would later confess that our Russia trip stretched even their concept of how to tackle a God-sized project.

Like many parents, we made it a priority to teach our children respect and tolerance for other cultures. We wanted them to experience the richness that comes from traveling and exploring other countries.

So what were we to do when our oldest daughter, a sophomore in high school, came home from youth convention and told us she had the opportunity to travel to Russia on a people-to-people exchange?

Really? Her first big trip without us? And half-way around the world to a place no one we knew had ever visited! What was she thinking?

This was the result of praying for her to have a meaningful experience at youth convention. . . .

We took a few deep breaths, listened to her passionate plea, and looked at all the ramifications. Those included funding, travel and time off school. We hesitantly stuck our parental feet in the water of trust. We knew her youth pastor/tour guide was utterly reliable. We understood her desire to learn and grow, and we respected the voice of the Spirit in her heart.

So where to begin?

Since the trip logistics were largely out of our hands except for the monumental task of fund raising, we began with baby steps. First we met with her school principal to explain her request for missing several days of school. He was wholeheartedly in favor of the experience. All her teachers granted their permission--as long as she brought back reports and filled in missing assignments.

First bridge crossed.

Then began the fund raising. Everything in us disliked the idea of asking friends for assistance. On the other hand, we knew the trip could not happen if the money had to come out of our one-income budget. Mark Shaner organized a fund-raising campaign and the letters to family and friends went out. Slowly but surely, the funds began to filter in. Every positive response was a faith-builder.

One of the first responses came from Melanie's great uncle, a dairy farmer whose heart had always been tender to missions. He was quite impressed with the team's goals for foreign exchange and wanted to encourage their youthful ambitions. So, he sold a dairy cow and sent her the $200 tithe. She and we were overwhelmed with his generosity.

Over the intervening months up to departure, Melanie's financial goals were met.

Another bridge crossed.

There would be plenty of bridges to cross before our departure. For instance, I knew it would be harder for me to raise funds for the trip than the students, because many donors incorrectly assumed that the South Lake Wales Church would pay my way. I had to find my own way across the fund-raising bridge.

Vickie and I had been putting money in a car replacement fund against the day our current car died. Before going to Ed Nelson to ask his permission to lead the team, I asked Vickie if she would let me use this money to invest in the Kingdom. I told her that I thought it would be easier for the students to raise funds than it would be for me as a youth pastor.

I once heard a quote attributed to Leonard Ravenhill that kept coming to my mind. "The opportunity of a lifetime must be seized within the lifetime of the opportunity." I told Vickie that I wanted to take advantage of this opportunity, whatever it cost. We had saved about $2,000 for a new car. It was our total family savings at that point. Vickie agreed to let me use it all, and that gave me the confidence to plunge ahead.

Our strategy for raising funds centered on "stock certificates." Each one carried the picture of each student, a short bio and our stated objective: for each team member to personally deliver 12 Bibles to Russia and share Jesus Christ with one Russian citizen. We then asked people to purchase $15 "shares" in the project. Those who purchased shares would in turn receive two letters from the Soviet Union–a big deal in those days--photos from the trip and a tape-recorded diary. Upon our return, we extended an invitation to each shareholder to a reception where they would hear reports about the dividends that their investment had produced.

Like everything we do in the Kingdom of God, the dividends rolled in in unexpected ways.

Sara Fasel attended Burns Avenue Church of God (later renamed High Point) in Lake Wales. She promised, and later delivered, a typed copy of the journal she kept during the trip to each of her stockholders. Years later, when Sara came across a copy of that Chelyabinsk journal and read what she had written about the USSR as a 15-year-old, she described it as "hilarious."

"It's sort of like watching the *Mortified* documentary," she said. Nevertheless, that journal was key to providing the necessary resources for Sara to go to Siberia.

Ron Hosey, youth pastor at First Church of God in Bradenton, threw his influence behind the effort to raise $3,000 to send Karis Blunden to Chelyabinsk. The Blundens, like most families in their circumstances, could not spare that kind of money. Ron became Karis's chief spokesman and most effective fund-raiser.

One day an elderly lady in the church gave Karis a large jar of small change. She said she had been saving it for years. The jar contained over $100.

Greg Campbell wouldn't remember where all his money came from, but he would always attribute the success of his efforts at fund raising to one important factor: the prayers of South Lake Wales church, especially those of George and Margaret Kickasola.

We were set to depart on April 10, 1991, from the Orlando International Airport. As the departure date drew nearer, we organized training events in preparation for the trip, spending entire days together at South Lake Wales church to learn basic phrases in Russian and orient ourselves to the culture.

Then the day finally came to say goodbye to families and friends. Several parents were at the airport to see us off. Among them was Mary Jane Newcomer.

"Some of the students traveling in the group were completely new to each other," she remembers. "We stood in a circle and prayed for this extraordinary group of students and leaders setting out for the Soviet Union. Our parental hearts prayed not only for safe travels, but for friendships. We asked that both within the group and with their Russian counterparts, they would become knit together in mutual love and respect."

As we boarded the plane heading for New York, Moscow and Chelyabinsk, we felt we were finally ready.

But nothing could have prepared us for what awaited.

Diary, April 21

At 2:30 a.m. we climb into our beds to awaken at 8 o'clock for a visit to Russia Mineral Museum and Folk Dome. Although it is Sunday, a church service is not on our agenda. The Russians are so accommodating they would probably have planned one, had we asked. I'm simply amazed at all of the warmth and hospitality! It's a beautiful day, and we have awakened ready to begin. Breakfast at 9:00, then our first shower in 38 hours. Oh how refreshing!

The lake outside is thick with ice, only about six feet next to the shore is thawed. Galena, a teacher and one of the Russian women in charge of discipline, went swimming in the sub-30-degree water. I can hardly believe it!

I have never in my entire life been given more gifts in two days: posters of Gorbachev, Yeltsin pins, honorary membership in the Chelyabinsk Police Force (along with a pin for my hat and an expensive pen marking graduation from the Police Academy), a police medal and a beautiful watch.

We have porridge for breakfast, along with pancakes, jelly, tomato juice and cranberries. The food is very good. I eat with a Russian teacher and we talk of problems in the USA and problems in the USSR. Kids in the USA have money and are not happy. Kids in the USSR have no money and are not happy. A real open door to share Jesus. Tomorrow I will present my first Bible to Albert, the literature teacher in Lyceum #31. We share more deeply each day--and it's only the second day!

This morning we traveled to the Nature Reserve in the Ural Mountains where many precious stones and gems are found and on display. Rubies, sapphires, granite, quartz and much, much more. I understand it is every geologist's dream to visit the place. I purchased a large round piece of fluoride (green) quartz for my desk. I was the last one to leave the museum for the bus and over 30 small children followed me as if I was an extra special oddity! They practiced some English, "Hello. How are you?" and I, Russian, "Я в порядке" (I am fine). To see their curiosity, hunger and deep respect was very moving!

We board the bus and Galena moved girls next to boys, and boys next to girls to encourage relationships. We introduce ourselves to one another over the bus's microphone. I ask for stamps and we stop at a large post office. They have only enough stamps to send 12 postcards – they definitely were not prepared for our big purchase. The hosts bought us stamps, 51 *coppetts* to send a postcard, two cents in American money.

We arrived back at the retreat center to eat lunch. The team met at 3:30 to hear what relationships are developing. We watched a video documentary about Karlana Stone and the Russian circus man and cried. The joy was incredible.

Diary, April 22

A new day begins and the weather is beautiful! Today we travel to Lyceum #31 in Chelyabinsk, where students have been waiting for our visit for some six months, the first Americans ever to come here.

On the way, Helen presented me with a book by Tolstoy for my children, a take-off of *Pinocchio*. We talked about families and wrote down names in their Russian and English equivalents.

State control is tight here and a person must carry his papers at all times. A citizen, for instance, can go study in Moscow, but if not studying or marrying, must return home.

We arrived at Lyceum #31 and were instant celebrities. Hundreds of children grades 4 to 11 surrounded us. The teachers who traveled with us were curious for us to meet their students, particularly their favorite students. Russian TV cameras were filming it all.

We went up to an English class and were very, very impressed by the children as they carried on simple conversations--and some quite complex for a foreign language speaker. We asked them questions and they answered quite well. The older students in grades 9 to 11 then carried on an in-depth conversation on ecology, which is also a problem in the USSR. They spoke English very well. They presented us with gifts and we, them.

I notice black dots on the map and learn they mark locations blocked from the view of orbiting satellites. The Russian TV cameras were present all along to record this historic occasion.

Quickly we were ushered off to another class where 11th graders, all top students at Lyceum #31, sat around tables with us. We ask questions of each other about the States, drug problems, what to do on a date, about school, after-school jobs, and so forth. They gave us beautiful gifts. Olga gave me a gift of a little wooden doll and asked me to write to her.

Children were pressing against glass doors to see us as we went from class to class. We were ushered out of the school onto a bus bound for Chelyabinsk Institute. This is a college of some 30,000 students. We went up to the fourth floor of a building for a reception with the school's English Department. Veteran professors sat stunned and listened in awe to us talking, amazed that they could actually understand us. They had learned English in a vacuum. We spoke American adolescent slang, a different dialect than the formal King's English they had learned.

They offered us a tennis match and appeared very curious about our lifestyle. I watched amazed as four college professors gathered around Greg Campbell, a ninth-grader, to learn from him.

We went to Chelyabinsk Town Square where only a month earlier demonstrators had lassoed a huge statue of Stalin and pulled it down. They had just found out how many Russians he had killed and refused to let the statue stand.

I should say a word about the economy. On April 2, officials raised the price of everything. One American dollar is now equivalent to 27 rubles, and people are struggling. The lines to buy shoes or bread are three to four hours long. Americans are into success. Russians are into survival.

Many positive signs exist though. A small green building covering one-third of a block houses the local Communist party. A huge building, covering a whole block, serves as headquarters for the Democratic Party and *Glasnost*, the name of the "openness movement" meant to bring about stable but necessary economic and social change. Only five years ago, the Communist party resided in this larger building.

Tonya, an English teacher in Lyceum #31, says there is still no Glasnost today. Russia has come a long way, but still no Glasnost yet. She had to have the KGB stamp our visas. She did not hide her frustration and hatred for the system.

Back at the retreat center Albert presented me with a pop-up book that tells a Russian folk story. Lunch came at 4:30 p.m., but very good regardless. The teams prepared a program for the TV cameras. We sang songs and performed skits, poems, dances, and several Russian games. (To the left, two times, then to the right, two times. Walk and walk, walk and walk. Heel to toe, halfway around, heel to toe and pass her down.) We rested, then ate again at 7:00 p.m. I will gain weight on this trip.

TV crews interviewed David Stone for a program to be aired while we are here. Had a dance, then time for another tea. Talked about friendships and the weeping that will come when it comes time to leave. The memories warm our hearts!

Celebrated Tanya's birthday at 1:00 a.m. with caviar, Russian chocolate, tuna on bread and cake. I wrote postcards before going to bed at 3:00 a.m. Tomorrow we paint our faces for a parade. Talk about interesting!

* * *

"Interesting" can mean many things in the English language, some good, some, well . . . interesting. Our students encountered many different kinds of "interesting" things during their introduction to the Soviet Union and its distinctive culture.

Karis Blunden's first impression of the Moscow airport was eerie silence. Most people were friendly enough, but bore a kind of depressed look. To Karis, everything looked old and dull. Clothing styles and interior décor made her feel as if she had stepped back in time. However, the impression of dullness could have been because of the long grip of the Siberian winter that was still evident. Karis had lived her entire life in Florida and never experienced drab winters.

The 1960s vintage buildings looked dark and old to the eyes of the Florida youth, not entirely unlike "up north" cities in the United States. The Russian people themselves looked older than their age, perhaps a result of smoking too many cigarettes from youth onward.

Our hosts spared no expense when it came to feeding us their favorite dishes. But we Americans simply could not rise to the challenge of finishing the meals they served up. Way too many courses came our way, heaped on plates much too loaded to consume in their entirety.

Russian food was particularly hard for Karis, a picky eater at that age. It seemed to her the cooks served mystery meat each night. Delicacies included a wiggly gelatinous mold with an entire fish encased inside. Turkey legs stuffed with ingredients we never were able to identify. Roast meat, cucumbers, sour cream and cake were often on the breakfast menu, along with potatoes, potatoes, and more potatoes.

The students soon relegated boney fish and mineral water to the "gross" category. One time in Moscow the group had the opportunity to try famous Russian caviar. Greg Campbell flat out declined the opportunity.

Russians do not take ice in their water, but when they learned that Floridians did, they produced generous supplies of ice at every meal. They were also very generous with their chocolate, of which they were unapologetically proud.

We tried to reciprocate with American delicacies. Karis Blunden had brought a jar of peanut butter along from the States. She learned, to her utter disbelief, that Russians had never eaten this staple food, so one night she let them try it. They thought it was awful! Interesting.

Melanie Newcomer's family did not drink alcohol, so she had never tasted liquor in her life. On her first visit to a Russian home, her host family brought out a lavish cake, a bottle of wine and proceeded to toast each other while intoning, "Long live our friend, Melanie!" Sensitive to their guest's scruples, however, the family served Melanie tea with her cake, much to the young lady's relief.

Culinary culture shock was not the only variety our students experienced. One day the group attended a Russian fashion show and were horrified that the models' armpits were unshaven.

Ideas about acceptable dress, or undress, as the case may be, differed markedly on that side of the Atlantic. On a visit to a public swimming pool, the American girls looked through a window in the shower room door to see the Russian women inside, including their tour group leaders, walking around completely naked "without a care in the world!" as Melanie recounted it.

Their hosts later introduced the girls to the Russian sauna. Upon arrival, they directed the guests to disrobe one by one and lie down uncovered on a spa bench. Then they massaged the girls all over with herbs before plunging them into a cold shower.

Once, a Russian boy named Max struck up a conversation with Melanie on the bus by asking, "Do you act like a baby sometimes?" Taken aback by what seemed to her a very personal question, but not wanting to miss a rare opportunity to talk to the shy young man, Melanie asked just what Max meant by that. "You know," he stammered, "do you ever tell stupid jokes?"

Actually we did tell some stupid jokes. Cross-cultural humor is difficult to pull off correctly, some jokes are simply non-translatable. For instance, Russian women feel genuine, wholesome affection for one another and are not as hung up as Americans about demonstrating their emotions in public. I once made a joke about this--an innocent joke, I thought--but the ladies were deeply offended.

One night David Stone was in a playful mood and sang "The Lion Sleeps Tonight," substituting Alexander's name. "In the jungle, the mighty jungle, Popov sleeps tonight." We Americans laughed at what we considered a friendly, even admiring, comic routine. Alexander did not laugh. We later learned the song totally embarrassed him.

Despite the miscues and misunderstandings, we managed to get along well with each other, partly because the Russians were so kind and generous, partly due to a conscious effort to put aside any annoyance.

"We were all getting a little aggravated at always being bombarded by questions," Sara Fasel later recalled. "The Russians really wanted to know what we are like, but the questions made us feel uncomfortable. But this feeling passed within a day or two, after I decided to try to be myself around them so they would get a real picture of Americans."

We formed genuine friendships with our hosts and they with us. Greg Campbell even fell hopelessly in love--for the very first time in his young life--with a Russian girl. "I had it bad," he admitted to me years later. "We wrote back and forth for months. It was a big deal to me."

Love is always a big deal, of course. Especially the kind of love Jesus talked about, such as loving your enemies and doing good to those who do you evil. I came to realize that if we could fall in love with one another, maybe we wouldn't spend so much time and money devising ways to kill each other.

Diary, April 23

Another day in the USSR and it's Shakespeare's birthday! After breakfast our hosts finished making masks and put them on our students in honor of Shakespeare. I videoed the proceedings, grateful to avoid painting my face. Got out of that one!

The TV camera crew is still here and asked to interview me about my job. This ought to be good. On public television, through an interpreter, I give my testimony and tell how I teach the Bible to students in America. They are fascinated.

As we spoke of peace and positive change, one of the reporters shared her concern that many people in the USSR have had dreams shattered so many times they have quit dreaming. I pointed out that John F. Kennedy, Martin Luther King Jr., and Abraham Lincoln were all dreamers, and paid the price. They all died young, but change happened. Her closing words were, "It is good to meet a dreamer from another country."

This program will be aired throughout the Chelyabinsk region on April 28 or 29, with over one million people watching. Potentially powerful!

All of the USA/USSR delegation joined for a parade of masks. They paraded as couples in the outdoor gazebo on the lake. Each told of their masks, performed a little dance called "The Froggy Doggy" and just had fun together. Played a big game of Russian football, which we call "soccer" in America. The USSR beat USA 7-0 in Ice Hockey. As we compete in sports with one another, it seems to open up relationships.

After lunch the teachers from Lyceum #31 arrived by train for a group lesson on poetry. We heard a number of Shakespeare works quoted. They also acted out works of George Bernard Shaw. Each American tried reading a Russian phrase such as, "can't see past his nose," and then gave an English translation. After each attempt we had to say "*Ya low blue vas* (I love you)." Had a lot of fun!

We had a team meeting to pray together and share our joys and concerns. Then dressed for the theater in Chelyabinsk.

Instead of sleeping on the two-hour bus ride into Chelyabinsk, I decided to "work the crowd," as Ed Nelson would say." I'm so glad I did. I started out in the front of the bus and as I made my way to the back seats, I was overwhelmed by the conversations. I talked with a geography teacher while one of the students interpreted. We talked of jobs and family, intrigued by each other's language. Tonya asked if I would be so kind to converse with two other English teachers further back on the bus.

We spoke of the church and they mentioned the increased attendance at the Orthodox church in Chelyabinsk. But only one church for a million people. According to them, the church is "traditional and ritualistic." I shared my testimony and how Jesus brings freedom. "It's not a ritual, but a relationship," I said. They are so hungry.

They also spoke of how they had been taught that Americans were cold and unloving, and how they realized this was not true. "We were taught the same about the USSR," I said, adding, "The hunger and desire is the same over there as here."

The bus ride could have gone on for many more hours as far as I was concerned. The Russians spoke of a lack of a way to teach values to their children, of no basis for moral grounding. Their hunger for a foundation is unbelievable. I could not quite believe that I was having this conversation, in Siberia, with Russian educators. What an opportunity!

We enjoyed the theatrical production--all in Russian--and then indulged in Russian ice cream and cake. I was so exhausted by then that I slept on the bus home. Arrived there at 12:00 a.m., for supper. As I write this, it's now 1:40 a.m., 5:40 p.m. in Florida. I'm missing my family very much!!

But what a day to sow seeds for Jesus in the USSR.

Diary, April 24

I awoke, wrote more postcards to our supporters back home, and headed for breakfast. Afterward we loaded up to go to the coal mines, but it was raining so three miles down the road we turned back. Spent the entire day playing *Uno*, chess, ping pong, billiards, flying kites, sleeping and singing songs and swapping stories with David Stone.

Had a great conversation with Alexia, a young Russian student who traveled to Shreveport. We talked of politics, comparing Gorbachev and Yeltsin. Yeltsin wants to strengthen local governments, Gorbachev wants to keep power centralized. Gorbachev feels pressure from the KGB and Communist Party and so is backpedaling on Glasnost. Alexia expressed his confidence in Yeltsin.

It turned into a day to build relationships and slow down the pace. Tomorrow is my birthday, so the whole day I was getting my head measured and showing pictures of Gina and Zach. They wanted to see my passport and visa. I'm sure tomorrow will be a big surprise!!

We were given an opportunity by Alexander Popov to take a Russian mathematics test and receive math lessons. Also, the KGB granted permission for us to stay Friday or Saturday night in family homes. This should be a real treat.

As we shared these opportunities with the American delegation, Shawn appeared very reserved about staying in homes. It was a pure culture shock for him, to the point of feeling uneasy almost to tears. I left the subject on hold to give time for us to process. It should be a great opportunity.

After a good supper, we attempted a conversation with a man out front who had had too much to drink. I was concerned because I thought he was after a fight. We avoided that, thankfully. Students spent the evening mingling with their hosts. I played some more pool with students and went upstairs for yet another tea.

Evidently I was 30 minutes late arriving and it broke Galena's heart, because she wanted to start celebrating my birthday early. At 12:15 a.m. they sang "Happy Birthday," and gave me a gift. They shared a common Russian birthday saying about "the candle is burning." Galena brought out Tarot cards, wanting to tell my future. I consented with much reservation. It turned out very fake--nothing about it that one could not otherwise figure out with common sense.

I know there is a big celebration on for tomorrow with me on stage and everyone else in the audience. I fall asleep quite anxious about what tomorrow holds.

Diary, April 25

Today is my birthday. At 1:00 a.m., I begin to write in my journal about a very full day and a very full past week. I reflect on open doors to speak, like with the TV reporter who shared that people in the USSR have dreamed for so long, and been let down, that she is afraid they have stopped dreaming. "It's good to meet a dreamer from another country!" she had said.

On the way to Chelyabinsk for the theater we spoke in the back of the bus with the English teachers. Vera Igoryevna spoke of the great hunger for spiritual things. As I revealed to her my relationship with God, her eyes inferred yearning for a relationship with her Creator. Sasha said that when the country falls apart, as it is currently doing, what do we fall back on? Nothing.

God, help me tell these stories, and not just events, when I return home.

My birthday began with a humming of *Happy Birthday* in the hall at 8:30 a.m. As I opened my door, four Russian women greeted me with a kiss on each cheek, a ribbon and whistle to call if I needed something or just felt like it. They had hung a beautiful banner on the door that stated their love for me, with Vickie, Gina, Zach and I holding hands. They sang Russian love songs as they invited me to go to the lake for a swim. The lyrics were a little scary. "In a room full of men, I fall in love with a married one," and "Beautiful men have a difficult time loving bad." Then we headed for the lake.

When we arrived, Everett and Shawn attempted to throw me in. Talk about scary! We watched a man fishing on the ice. We spoke to him and he showed us a fish he had caught, demonstrating how he catches them with bait and a slip knot. Amazing!

We walked back to the house, enjoying the beautiful forest. I showered and again was greeted at my door, this time with a knight outfit made of cardboard: breastplate, shield, sword and helmet. They put it on me and then gave me another knight costume for Zachariah packed in a box. Hope I can figure out the instructions (in Russian) to assemble it once I get home. Ha! I went to breakfast in the cardboard armor. What a neat thing! They had fixed a plate of spaghetti especially for me.

After breakfast, Max presented me with a Soviet hat and a book with a card and beautiful pictures inside. What a neat hat! Alexia then gave me a shirt worn by military pilots, given to him by his grandfather. What an honor! I immediately put it on. I wore it downstairs and they gave me shoulder stripes to go with it. A policeman gave me a military police hat and Sasha gave me a perfect policeman medal. Helen gave me more stripes and on and on until I was completely outfitted as a pilot. I cannot believe this generosity!

Helen earns 350 rubles and her husband Sasha makes 500 rubles. That's a total of 850 rubles or $32 dollars a month, in a country where it costs 650 Rubles for a pair of Pony brand tennis shoes and 600 rubles for a pair of jeans. How do they make it? And still they have given me gift after gift after gift.

Olga and Victoria gave me more than a dozen beautiful Russian Yellow Snowdrop flowers. Edward presented me with a Don Quixote doll. Very nice! Another person gave me a painter's hat with a medallion. Two guys gave me five ruble coins-- collector items. Wow! I am awed at their generosity. What a birthday!

We played tennis and also a couple of Russian games, counting games mostly. One has you clap on any multiple of three you come to in a word. We played some animal game they said was an American game, but I had never played it.

They presented me with a birthday cake at lunch and again sang *Happy Birthday*. Our American students had baked the cake with Kostya's help as interpreter. The Russians were amazed. They had never seen an instant cake mix. You just add water! It came in a box my wife had secretly slipped to the students before we left Florida. What a treat! Thanks, Vickie. I love my wife so much and think of her all the time.

After lunch, we dressed up big-time and headed for the city to meet with all the city officials. They had the table set and waiting for us. The city council greeted us with open arms and, again, incredible hospitality! We learned that the city of Chelyabinsk is actually only 250 years old. Each student shared in the conversation and the adults were impressed by what they said and the questions they asked. They commented that, as people, we are the same, only our language and culture differ.

I met the director of 30 youth clubs in Chelyabinsk, each with 50 to 100 members. After the meeting, we went shopping. The stuff we bought was very cheap for us, but expensive for them. We bought envelopes at the post office and went to a toy store. It was like walking back to the 1920's, incredible! Helen acknowledged how bad things are and tried to make excuses. They are busy trying to survive over here while we bathe in success.

I chanced to meet a lovely lady in the department store who looks just like Joan Baez. We had earlier had a conversation on the bus. I later bumped into Helen's friend, Allah. What are the chances of this happening in a city of one million?!

Shawn Brown struck up a conversation with a stranger, telling the man about America. How this man wished his children could grow up in America.

Shawn gave him a key chain and the man wanted to give something back, but had nothing. So he gave Shawn sunflower seeds. Then the Russian Soviet delegation asked the man to leave. It broke Shawn's heart!

I tried to sleep on the bus as we headed back to the retreat center. An hour from home, I woke up and watched the barren landscape pass the window. I wondered how I could describe a country where people have so little to people in a country that has so much.

Kostya came down the aisle and sat next to me. He asked how it felt to be 29. I told him "the candle is burning," and that I must make a difference with my life. As I talked about our great wealth as Americans and how I have to learn to share when I return home, I wept. I was embarrassed by the disparity. Kostya said kindly, "Just be yourself." Nevertheless, we could make a difference if we so desired. To whom much is given, much is required.

Kostya seems very hungry for what we have, yet he respects us. Our conversation was purely on an emotional, rather than intellectual, level. He complimented me on being someone who understands cultures well, and said he wants to be like me. We continued to talk over supper. He is a great young man!

Oh Lord, please make my life a challenge, and not a compromise.

Our American team met afterward, and what a meeting it was. We have all watched so many doors open. We've seen a great hunger to hear about Jesus. Some students are telling their Russian hosts about Jesus very naturally. I am not believing what is happening. Awesome!

Had another tea with many toasts offered to the birthday boy. So many powerful statements--I wish I could record them all. Edward said that it seems we are really Russians, that we are only playing the role of being Americans. This is truly making us into a family. They gave me chocolate, a red helmet to remember them by, and a whistle to use in emergencies.

What a day!!

* * *

I would later discover that these long, adventure-packed days were merely the staging ground for long and serious conversations at night between our students and their new Russian friends. Inevitably, the discussions turned to spiritual matters.

One evening Melanie and Karis got into an intense conversation with a very articulate and sociable Olga "Smith." (We never did learn her real surname. Olga told us to call her that because her last name was too hard to pronounce, even for Russians.)

Olga asked tough intellectual questions about God and the Bible. She wanted to know about creation, end times, the Trinity, and so on. "Why didn't Jesus get married and have kids? Why did there need to be four accounts of Jesus' life?" Karis is the type of person who struggles to come up with answers on the spot, usually thinking of the right thing to say about two days after the conversation. But that night she had no trouble communicating. She could feel the Holy Spirit speak to the issues through her.

Coincidentally, her Bible class at the Christian high school she attended in Florida had recently studied the differences between the four Gospels and the uniqueness of each. Karis was able to recall this information and explain it to Olga. The answer to the question about Jesus' family life was completely Spirit-breathed. Karis had never in her young life considered this question before, but was able to satisfy Olga's questioning.

Olga was not the only one who felt the impact of the conversation that evening. At 15 years of age, Karis suddenly and joyfully realized that God could use her-- little ol' her, a shy teenager from Florida suffering from culture shock--to speak the truth.

Conversations turned serious when the subject of God or the Bible came up. Albert Akmalov, who taught literature to fifth-graders, said he had given his students lots of lessons on the Bible but always treated it as mythology that lacked any historical truth. Yet he had come to realize that atheism provided no basis for morality and ethics.

Albert told me he recalled his *babushka* (grandmother) reading the Bible to him as a small child, while hiding under the bed sheets together for fear they would be caught.

"The Russians demonstrated a desire to know, to seek, to ask," Melanie Newcomer said. "They often propelled conversation towards spiritual matters without any prompting on our part. Whether we were tucked into the corners of our dorm rooms or sprawled on the beds, the talk invariably led to the Bible."

The Florida team soon noticed that their Russian counterparts knew about the Bible and its contents in detail, perhaps even better than the Americans themselves. Yet it was a detached knowledge, a sterile, factual knowledge. They knew the Bible as one knows a Math book, memorizing facts, annotating data. "It was very two-dimensional, without the emotion and deeper understanding of what the stories taught and stood for," Melanie said.

One day Olga pointedly asked to talk with Karis and Melanie. The three sat down together and Olga began peppering the two Americans with questions about Christianity. "Why didn't Jesus have a son?" "What does the whole three-in-One thing mean?" The questions poured out with an intensity the two Christian teenagers had never experienced before.

Melanie began to pray, asking God to give her and Karis the right words to answer. They realized their own inadequacy in the moment. Olga became agitated at the noise level in their surroundings and frustrated that the language barrier muddled good communication. She wanted so much to understand, and listened intently as the trio read various scriptures.

After an hour, Olga said, "I feel a light in my heart and in my arm."

Melanie didn't know exactly what Olga meant by that, but was careful to note the quote in her diary so she could recall it later.

However, Melanie would never forget the words Olga spoke next. "When you came, I thought you would be like all other Americans, but now I think you are special. There are invisible roads between our hearts and invisible bridges between our minds."

The American girl's heart burned for her Russian friend to fully comprehend God's revelation.

I found out that God was setting other hearts afire in our group of students. Greg Campbell was witnessing the power of the Word every day in the conversations and experiences. It was during this trip that Greg began to read his Bible daily and systematically. It was a habit he would continue throughout life.

Diary, April 26

I'm getting used to the idea of being 29.

Our day began early with breakfast at 8:20 and a bus ride to the municipal pool. I sat with Victoria, the ninth-grade daughter of Alexander Popov, Headmaster of Lyceum #31. She told me her dad works seven days a week. She wishes he spent more time with her. Her mom raised her as an only child and she has turned into a very beautiful and interesting person! She asked me if I thought it strange that she did not have a boyfriend. "*Nyet!* That is a good thing at your age," I replied.

The municipal pool was very refreshing. Our group had a great time jumping off the high dive together. We have become like one large family. Our group presented a set of five inflating needles to the locker room attendants. It touched their hearts very much.

From there we went to a modeling agency and watched the rehearsal for an upcoming beauty pageant. Some very beautiful ladies doing aerobics, and even a break-dance. Two of our students taught them the Bus Stop and did the Jitterbug with them. They seemed awed by our presence, and took great delight in learning a dance from a group of American high school students. All very interesting.

Our hosts then treated us to the nicest restaurant in Chelyabinsk. We drank punch and coffee, and then we emptied two bowls each of Russian ice cream. The bathrooms had squatty-potties and we laughed and joked about that. I went to sleep on the bus home.

Once back at camp, Sasha went out and spent 350 rubles--equivalent to his wife's monthly salary--to buy oranges for our group. At lunch I sat with Galena's son, Alex, and enjoyed his company. He shared an insight about Americans not knowing how to amuse themselves and that's why TV and cinema dominate our leisure time. Later, I rode with Alex on a borrowed policeman's motorcycle into the woods through villages and out to the railroad tracks. We picked some flowers and listened to the music of the forest. Very beautiful!

We played soccer again and once again we Americans were beaten badly. Then Shawn played a Russian student in tennis and won!

Prior to our daily team meeting and supper, I watched as Victoria Popova studied the student Bible we gave her for an entire intense hour. A crowd gathered. How much better can it get?

The policeman brought me into his barracks and presented me with a police jacket. I was speechless. We are talking a *police jacket*! It must be very expensive.

What an honor. I had broken through the rough exterior of the four KGB officers. They even let me take pictures of them and their gun!

We Floridians held a team meeting. The adults were amazed at the conversations that the students are having about God, his Word and the power of a relationship with Jesus. Tomorrow we will ask the USSR students and adults who are interested to join our meeting at the table, in order to answer some of their many questions about the faith. What we are witnessing is beyond words. Awesome!

Ate supper with Alexia, a very interesting fellow who seems very proud of himself. I think he is trying hard to cover up his many fears about his country's current situation and the impression it is making on us Americans.

The radio said a bear had attacked and killed a hiker, and that people should not wander about in the woods alone. That was also interesting. I had joked of seeing a bear. Not so funny now.

We played some volleyball, then laid out gifts and a Bible. I want to present them to the police officer. The students are spending a lot of time together with their new Russian friends. At one point tonight while we were about to learn more Russian dances, Greg stopped the music and called everyone together. He shared that he had always been taught that Soviets were enemies of Americans, but that he has come to realize we are all the same.

Greg had met a lovely young lady and wanted to give her a special ring to symbolize eternal friendship. "For me? Oh, it's very expensive!" she said, and gave Greg a kiss.

Diary, April 27

Breakfast and off to the lake. I gave Andrew, the policeman and Andrei gifts in exchange for the jacket and hat that they had given me. Took a picture, then gave all three of them a Bible. What a time!

As I sit down to write tonight I have so many thoughts rushing through my mind that I do not know where to begin. I could start with the request from Kostya to send him 20 to 30 Bibles from America so that his language and linguistic class at the university could study conventional English.

Or I could tell of Helen's plans to teach an American game and sing "Father I Adore You" to her class. She expressed her feeling that people who sing this kind of song can do no wrong.

Maybe I could write about Victoria, another 18-year-old freshman at the university. She said she is searching for a better understanding of God and that a still small voice leads her to do right and wrong. She is not a Christian, yet experiences God in many of the same ways as I.

Or I could talk about our stop in Miass at the village store where they literally had nothing for sale. People can only purchase one bag of macaroni noodles a month. The purchase is marked on a ration card. If they buy any food at a supermarket, it costs 10 times as much.

I could tell about how our shocked reaction and their realization of their country's plight brought tears to their eyes. Embarrassed by this, Helen and Galena wept.

Or I could tell of my emotional conversation later with Helen, which Kostya translated. He expressed embarrassment for Helen's tears. She said she did not want to put their nation's problems on my shoulders! Our friendship with the Soviet people has grown so deep.

Abraham Maslow's hierarchy of needs theory makes more sense to me now than ever before. We have met a basic human need, built a friendship, warmed up to one another and are coming closer to the most important issue of life. Everyone here is seeking! Albert and Kostya both want private conversations all the time. The government may have cancelled glasnost in the rest of the country, but it still operates here!

We sang the words to the song, "Make my life a challenge Lord, Make me very wise," before we went to see the second most beautiful lake in the Soviet Union. We walked in the icy water and on the ice itself. We enjoyed a picnic and I shared some more with Victoria about God and the Bible. Then we played kickball and started back to the camp.

We passed through the factory district where they make the USSR's missiles. We were told that people who do business with the military must give 80 percent of the profit to Moscow. Ironically, it takes 80 percent of one's income just to survive day-to-day.

The Communists have lied to the people here for so long. They assure them that they are the best, the strongest, the biggest; the best in dance, sports and circus arts. Now they are finding that what they have been told is not necessarily true, and it has taken the heart out of the people.

We returned to the camp to play volleyball, wash clothes and eat supper. At our daily team meeting I told the kids, "Today we crawled into the Russians' culture just a bit, and I hurt with them." I want so badly to go home and create a desire to help.

We had tea, again. David Stone remarked at that first tea that "we should do this every night," and they took him up on it! So it's tea, every night.

Tomorrow is Sunday. We will invite the group to join us at a worship service on a voluntary basis. This is going to be a reach-out service. So many questions, so little time to answer.

* * *

Our brief time at the store in Miass, I would come to realize, was a huge turning point in the relationship between us and our Russian hosts. It was the moment when things got real, very real, for all of us. And it opened a door for the Holy Spirit to move in a way which could never have been planned.

Once we had taken stock of the bare shelves and stark rations at the Miass grocery, our Russian friends quickly ushered us out of the store. The students began boarding the bus, but I noticed the Russian teachers walking away from the group. Then I saw that they were weeping.

Back on the bus, I asked Albert Akmalov, a literature teacher at Lyceum #31, "How long has it been like this?" I expected an answer something like, "Since last October, when the prices soared. But understand, this is not indicative of the entire country."

But instead Albert said, "It's been like this since the Revolution of 1917. Statisticians predict that, before the end of this year, there will be mass starvation."

I was quiet as I pondered this possibility. Then Albert added quietly, "The only thing that will change Russia is if we let God back into our country."

His reply made me resolve to fetch one of the Russian Bibles from my room as soon as we arrived back at the center, present it to Albert and share Jesus Christ with him. After all, each Florida group member had made a commitment to their sponsors back home to personally deliver 12 Bibles and share Jesus Christ with at least one person while in Russia.

So I wrote a note inside the cover of one of the Russian Bibles that simply said, "This book changed my life and I believe it can change yours, too," and presented it to Albert. "This is a great book for a literature teacher," I quipped. He expressed deep gratitude for the gift.

But as usual, God had a bigger plan.

After dinner that night, David Stone and I pulled the team of 11 Americans into a room for a critical meeting. We had noticed the Florida students going to bed very late, night after night, and rising extremely early every morning. We decided it would be prudent to remind them of the importance of getting good sleep and taking advantage of every opportunity to rest, in order to prevent anybody from getting sick so far from home.

"We would sleep more if we could," the students told us, "but the Russians want to talk. They have constant questions about what we believe and who Jesus Christ is. They want to know about our churches. They ask all kinds of questions about Christianity and what it means to us."

David Stone and I looked at each other and knew that instructions about getting enough sleep would not only be futile, but counterproductive to what God was doing in and through the students. God's Spirit was moving in the hearts and minds of the students and teachers as these private dialogues occurred. The conversation went from urging the American group to get proper rest to thanking God for what He was doing in the lives of our Russian hosts. We sang and prayed together, asking God to continue to use us in the few days that remained of our visit.

We left the room in a cheerful mood to go back and hang out some more before turning in for the night. We found several of the Russian delegation waiting. They had yet another question for us.

"What happens to you Americans when you go into that room together?" they asked. "You go in one way, but you come out another way. You change."

Their observation cheered us even more. It had not dawned on us that as we spent time with one another sharing the Word and praying together, God was working a noticeable transformation in our inner being.

Our answer to this question was actually a suggestion. "Tomorrow is Sunday," we said. "Since this was a cultural exchange trip, we ought to show you what we do in our culture on Sunday mornings."

"Why don't we all meet in the assembly hall for a worship service? That way you can catch a glimpse of American culture, at least the Christian part of the culture."

They agreed that such an experience fit with the purpose of our cultural exchange. We invited everybody who was interested to join us for worship, purely voluntary.

The next morning, every single Russian would gather in the Assembly Room--students, teachers, policemen, cooks, as well as the headmaster of Lyceum #31--for our impromptu church service.

Diary, April 28

Awoke this morning to write postcards and eat a great breakfast with Igor, one of the Soviet students. Then we went into the assembly hall for Sunday worship. Talk about awesome! God's Spirit was at work and He needs no visa!

We began with people coming in quietly and taking their seats while David led us in song. Shawn Brown stood to pray, and then I read Philippians 2:3-11 and made some comments about Jesus' life. Kostya interpreted. I pointed out that if Jesus lived today, He would not be found in Washington D.C., Moscow, Leningrad or Kiev, but among the common people. He chose his followers from ordinary folk, not to change the world from the top down, but from the bottom up.

Then a member of our delegation, Stephanie, sang a contemporary version of *Amazing Grace*. David Stone pointed out that God orders our life in amazing ways, that He can bring people together even out of tragedy. He told the story of his daughter, Karlana, and how through her accident and injury we were there at that moment. He said, "So now we are going to have what I call a Reach Out Service. If someone wishes to say something, raise your hand. I will point to you and you can talk about whatever you want. You can share a joy or express a concern, make a comment or ask a question about anything."

Everett Grayson shared that he began this trip in North Carolina with a family of three to love. Then in New York, he met up with a family of 11 to love. And now in Chelyabinsk he has a family that is more than he can count to love. His wife Pat shared that she had never experienced God's presence so strongly as she did today! Meg Grayson then said how in a few short days we would leave, maybe never to see each other again. But although we will be miles apart, our hearts will bring us together.

Galena shared how worshippers burn candles in churches in the USSR. "The flame only leaves ashes," she observed, "but we have lit a fire in our hearts that will never go out!"

Olga confessed that all her life she thought she was happy, but now she knows that something has been missing. She knows what this is now, and she is truly happy!

I admitted that I expected to develop mere surface relationships on our visit. "But both of our delegations have opened our hearts to each other," I said. "That comes with a risk, because open hearts are vulnerable. Yet, our relationships now run very deep!"

Mosha started crying because her grandfather died one week ago. Tears followed from members of both delegations as many more people shared their thoughts. I can't remember everyone who spoke, but the comments went something like, "All my life I have looked for peace and joy, and this morning I have found real peace and real joy." Or, "All my life I have searched for happiness, and this morning I have found true happiness."

God's presence was obvious in the room. I finally closed the service by explaining that, at the end of these worship times in our country, we ask persons to come to the front of the room to speak with God as a friend, and invite Him to come into their lives.

The next few minutes were amazing. We watched Russian teachers and students come to the front to ask God to fill this hole in their lives. There were tears of joy and expressions of freedom. I personally prayed with Galena and Alex and Victoria. Galena said we must do this every morning so when we leave we will be closer to God!

Before it was over, everyone had come up front with the exception of the headmaster of Lyceum #31 and the four policemen, who had positioned themselves along the side of the room. The last two people to leave the assembly room were the headmaster's daughter, Vica, who could not seem to stop the tears, and me. I wondered to myself what the headmaster, the man who had extended the invitation to us originally, was thinking after observing a cultural exchange trip develop into a spiritual revival.

On our walk up the five flights of stairs to where we were staying, we met the headmaster on his way down. Alexander Popov said something to his daughter in Russian, asking her to translate, and I realized that I was about to find out what the headmaster was thinking.

"Tell Mark that all my life I have been taught to think with my head, and this morning I have learned that I need to begin to think with my heart."

* * *

The rest of that Sunday resembled pretty much every other day of our cultural exchange. After the remarkable worship service, we boarded the bus and headed for Chelyabinsk and the circus. We took some luggage with us this time, because our group would stay in people's homes tonight. Helen and her husband

Sasha would host me. The three of us were very much looking forward to the experience.

The circus was great, especially watching the anticipation in people's eyes as every performance seemed more daring than the previous one. Natasha, one of the teachers I had met, gave me the names and pictures of 20 children and asked that I make them my pen pals. Then she presented me with a semiprecious stone for my wife Vickie, a scarf for daughter Gina and a toy truck for Zach. I later gave her a Bible, coffee and sewing needles in return. Natasha's eyes filled with tears at this.

I joined Sasha and Helen and we walked through this great city. My new friends had welcomed us so warmly. I felt something like an American-Russian at this point.

We took an elevator to the seventh floor apartment where Helen's mom lived. This is the place where we would spend the evening. It was a bit small and somewhat dingy in comparison to Florida apartments, but comfortable, nicely furnished and solidly middle-class by Soviet standards. It was such a treat and joy to have this experience! I was introduced to Helen's mother, who looked at me blankly as I tried to converse with her through Sasha. Actually, I had to rely more on hand signals, charades and smiles than words. The family then presented me with yet more gifts for Vickie, Gina and Zach. I am not believing the gifts.

We dined on caviar, sausage, and noodles with meat sauce. Russian ice cream and chocolate cake came with tea for dessert. Meanwhile, Helen explained the shopping card system to me, which grants a monthly ration to each citizen of staples such as 10 eggs, three pounds of meat and so forth. I thought I was poor, but no way could I live on $32 a month like these folks are expected to do.

Two pediatricians, Alle and Slava, joined us for the evening. Along with school teacher Helen and her historian husband Sasha, I could rely on informed perspectives on any number of topics of conversation. Our talk turned to politics, their dreams for their country, and our mutual desire for peace. We stayed up late talking about the whys and wherefores of American success, and if what they see in our movies is actually real! We took pictures and made some movies of our own, while laughing, joking and enjoying an unqualified good time.

Meanwhile, my students from Florida were having a time of their own, on their own, with other Chelyabinsk families. Greg Campbell got a glimpse into the long history of spiritual warfare while visiting a Russian Orthodox Church with his host family.

"We weren't there for a mass," he later told me. "We just went in, looked around, and lit a candle. I had a sense of oppression, of weight; I'm not sure what words to use. I could relate the atmosphere to other spiritual warfare experiences I'd had as a teen, both before and after that trip."

God was revealing to Greg other lessons about warfare. Up until his visit to Russia, he had chosen a career path that would lead him to join the Air Force. In fact, his strong patriotism was one of the factors that motivated Greg to travel to the Soviet Union in order to discover as many secrets as he could about America's Cold War rival.

But Greg had just made friends with several Russian students, including an attractive young woman. Tonight he even found himself the guest of a warm, generous Russian family. It dawned on him that he could never join the Air Force, where he might be asked to drop bombs on people who were his friends. Greg decided to redirect his career path.

Melanie Newcomer spent the night with Nastya and her family. The two girls had formed an instant and natural connection with each other from the moment they met, despite the fact that Nastya spoke little English and Melanie no Russian. Melanie's home stay experience produced some of her most precious memories of Chelyabinsk.

She later wrote an account of that evening to share with the team.

Fear tugged at my sensibilities as I drove off into a foreign city of more than one million with Nastya, whom I had only known one week. Her parents were entirely unable to communicate and I was clueless as to what I would experience in the next 24 hours.

George, a family friend who spoke English, accompanied us for part of the evening. Upon being introduced, he peered at me and immediately asked, "Are you really an American? This is an unusual circumstance." No greater understatement was ever spoken!

George was very eager to engage in conversations about the Bible and religion. He mentioned one of his friends who was interested in the 'Indian' religion--reincarnation, it seems--but told me he just didn't know what was right.

I chose to share how God was important to me and how He helps me in my life. George asked if I had a Bible he could buy. By this point in the trip, I didn't have any more Russian Bibles to give out. Instead of recognizing a great move of the Spirit-- perhaps due to a move of the spirits--I instantly began to struggle. You see, I had one English Bible left, but it was mine, a Bible special to me. If I gave it away, I wouldn't have any access to a Bible. At least, until I got back to the United States, where I could buy a Bible for every day of the week and every room of the house.

I am so glad I came to my senses quickly. "Here, George, I want to give this Bible to you," I said. At first he looked dazed, and then it seemed his eyes began to tear. I refused his offers to pay, but conceded, "Your gift to me is that you read it." I don't have words to describe the gift of his delight.

* * *

Diary, April 29
Awoke and had breakfast of caviar, sausage, etc. with Helen, then left for a walk through the city to the stores and market. The market was interesting. When other shoppers or shopkeepers found me to be an American, they wanted to be videoed with me. One merchant gave me an apple. I walked through a church that was being refurbished and learned that early in this century, there were 200 churches in the city. Now only two remain. Most were torn down. A Bible costs 78 rubles, very expensive when workers make only 350 rubles a month!

We visited Lyceum #109 to speak to English and Geography classes and to tour the school. We had a cup of tea with the principal, Eugene, and found out that Sasha is the assistant principal here. The school gave me a semi-precious jasper stone as a gift.

As I rode the bus and walked the streets, I felt myself to be almost Russian. Quite an experience! I met up with the rest of the group for a walk through a park and a visit to a ladies underwear factory and kindergarten. The kindergarten was awesome with little beds, puppet stages, tiny lockers, kindergarten-sized bathroom and a teacher very amazed to see us.

Once on the bus we headed for camp. Vica asked me some tough faith questions regarding her thoughts of God being a vengeful God or a God of love. After lunch, we had another team meeting to debrief our home stays and saw how God has used each of these students in a unique way. Melanie had given away her favorite Bible to a man and told us of his amazed response. Karis shared about giving a Bible to a lady whose response was similarly awe-inspiring.

An early supper tonight, 7:00 p.m. We watched ourselves on TV--the station has made a news series about our visit--and then I went for a walk with Steph and Alexia. Alexia is a boy hurting for someone to reach out to him. He's very critical and very empty. I pray something will happen quickly. The adults had a cookout by the lake, nine Russians and four Americans, sitting by the fire as friends, drinking juice and eating shish kabobs. The sky was beautiful. It ended with us singing "Father I Adore You."

We then went to the bath house and I had a real Russian bath. What an experience! We laughed and sang "Friends Are Friends Forever." We simply enjoy being with one another.

When I brought this group to the USSR, I thought we would plant a few seeds. I did not know we would plant 30 acres!

Diary, April 30
We leave tomorrow.

Emotion is already beginning to fill the air as we anticipate departure from Chelyabinsk. We will join in small discipleship groups tomorrow morning. God has birthed something bigger on this journey than any of us expected. I would love to baptize the folks who have trusted Christ, but must test my motives first. David Stone and I collected our thoughts on what we should do now, conscious of the fact that we are going back to the United States and may never return to Chelyabinsk. Our best wisdom suggested that Albert Akmalov, the Russian literature teacher who enjoys credibility among his peers, is our key man. We decided to ask Albert to lead a discipleship group that would meet in his classroom at Lyceum #31.

After breakfast, the group took a walk through the village and up a hill to see the mountains and lakes. A family invited us to their boat dock and summer home. They had cow's milk fresh that morning, tea, cooked apples and raspberry jelly. We had water fights, played on their boat and sang together. The grandmother of the family was 82 and cute as a button. The lake was beautiful, the people phenomenal. What an enjoyable time!

I invited Shawn and Greg to come along with Alex, Everett, Albert and myself to the bath house. These guys must have this experience. In keeping with custom intended to relax the muscles, Alex whipped us hard with tree branches. It's two days later as I write this and I can still feel the cuts in my skin. This sounds really harsh, but it's an experience unlike any other and very refreshing. We ate lunch and played football until 5:00. We had a meeting with everyone and put our signatures on about 60 postcards. We watched David Stone's interview on the TV news, and then dressed up for the evening meal. Then we dressed down for a final service, which centered on *koinonia*. Karis, Melanie, Everett and I put together gifts for every student and adult involved in the culture exchange.

After songs and prayer, I read 1 Corinthians 12:12-27 and shared some words. Then we gave our gifts. Everyone now had their own Bible, so we gave the leftover copies to Albert, the Russian Literature teacher. He will be very efficient at distributing them!

At 11:00 p.m. adult leaders left to have *chi,* tea. They took us to an exquisite room above the dining hall. It featured chandeliers and beautiful table settings. This would be our fifth meal in this 24-hour period. Sausage, cucumber, salad, hamburgers, pork chops, French fries and much, much more. I washed it down with about a gallon of water, as we drank toast after toast.

The chi went on until 1:00 a.m., with some more gift-giving thrown in. I started back to the room to pack, but the police lieutenant wanted to talk. Turns out he was born on April 25, 1962, at 12:15 Siberian time, and I was born the same day in Missouri at 3:15. We calculated that the two of us came into the world only one hour apart, sort of a USSR-USA set of twins. I could not believe this! We warmed to one another immediately. I learned his wife is Anna and they have a five-year-old boy.

It was 2:30 a.m. when I finally got back to the room. Started to pack but was too tired and fell asleep. Woke up at 6:00, packed and went back to sleep at 7:15 for a nap until breakfast at 8:00.

* * *

I had taken advantage of the farewell chi that final night to talk with Albert Akmalov about the follow-up plan David Stone and I had come up with.

"We suggest you assemble members of this delegation who are interested on Sundays in your classroom at Lyceum #31. Serve refreshments and study the Bibles we that have given you.

"We emphasize that you should not just read the Bibles for head knowledge, to satisfy intellectual curiosity, but examine the Scriptures one passage at a time, asking yourselves how you can apply this specific teaching to your everyday lives over the coming week.

"God wants to bring a new church to Chelyabinsk; one not filled with form and tradition, but a group of believers who will consistently study God's Word and learn to apply its truths to everyday life in Russia."

Then I gulped as I came to the main point of the appeal, wondering if I could follow through on the plan I was about to propose.

"If you will do this," I said, "I promise to regularly stay in touch by letter to encourage you. And . . . ," I took a deep breath, "I commit to return next year with another group of Christians to help you plant this new church in Chelyabinsk."

Albert looked at me silently for a moment, and then nodded. "I will do this," he said. Helen agreed to help translate letters and Kostya agreed to do whatever he could to support the project. God had planted a seed in all our hearts, it seemed. We felt strongly that we must water that seed and trust Him to make it grow.

* * *

May 1 was May Day, or International Worker's Day as it is known and observed in many European countries, but not in the United States. The reason behind the difference is the infamous Haymarket Affair that occurred in Chicago, Illinois on May 1, 1886. Somebody--no one knows for sure who--exploded a dynamite bomb during a peaceful workers' rally in support of the eight-hour work day. Seven police and four civilians died in the blast and ensuing gunfire. Even though the real culprit(s) was never apprehended, eight activists were convicted and four of them eventually hanged for the crime. When Congress unanimously voted to establish a federal holiday for American workers, following another deadly strike involving railroad workers in Chicago in 1894, President Grover Cleveland made sure it would not be celebrated on May Day. He feared the association with that date would rekindle the resentment associated with those dark chapters in U.S. history.

In the "worker's paradise" that was the USSR, May Day did not engender strikes or protest rallies. Instead, the holiday brought lots of parades and big crowds. We took our final drive through Chelyabinsk, headed for the airport through multitudes of May Day/Worker's Day celebrants lining the streets and parading down broad avenues. But the mood on the bus was anything but festive. No one said a word, in fact. It was as if we were afraid to speak, that if we expressed our feelings at this point, emotions would take over and we would be reduced to tears.

Upon arrival at the airport, our group went into a small room to await departure, which was not until 2:40 in the afternoon. That room soon began to fill with tears. Natasha, her son and a friend were present. She gave me yet another semi-precious stone, a book about the stones and another book about Mikhail Gorbachev. That reminded me that I wanted to buy stamps. On my way through the terminal to the post office, I called Sasha to say goodbye. That was tough enough. By the time I was back in the room, however, the tears were flowing freely, and I found myself blubbering with all the rest. We had become such close friends in such a short time, and now we were having to part company.

Some airport personnel came in, pushed our Russian companions out of the room and shut the door in their faces. And suddenly, that was that. Our students were weeping big time now. What a sudden and abrupt ending to our time together!

We were the first to board the plane to Moscow where, due to the time change, our two-hour flight arrived at exactly the same time we had taken off from Chelyabinsk. Natasha and Marina greeted us and we boarded the bus for the hotel, passing people working small plots of land in garden parks, a unique feature of European cities.

The hotel rooms were nice and we each had a private shower; no walking down 40 steps to get to it. Very pleasant! We relaxed before supper and I fell into bed at 8:30.

The next morning I got to talk to my wife. Talk about a great feeling! I love her so much! She is so beautiful, her voice so pleasant. She always brings great warmth and comfort to my spirit. I asked Vickie to call all of the students' parents and let them know we are safe. I couldn't wait to see her the following night in Orlando. I asked her to fix a typical American meal for my homecoming.

After breakfast we exchanged money that we spent on dolls and hats and other souvenirs at a local flea market. We enjoyed lunch at Pizza Hut, and then toured the Metro subway. We must have stopped at seven or eight stations, all very clean with extremely long escalators. I forgot that I was in Moscow.

I returned to the hotel for a catnap and rehash of the trip with David Stone. We concluded that nothing could have been improved; everything had happened so smoothly. The prayer warriors back home were making it tick! We thanked God for a marvelous experience.

I attempted to pack, but my heart was not in it. Due to a commitment to celebrate a wedding back in Florida, I would have to leave a day early to return to the United States. I dressed for the Bolshoi Theater where we were to see the greatest ballet company in the world perform. Scalpers out front sold us $30 tickets for only $11. Imagine! The theater was awe-inspiring and the ballet incredibly beautiful. I'm so glad I went.

Back at the hotel, I finished packing, put some necessary paperwork in order and said goodbye to the group. I so much regretted leaving the group a day early. On the other hand, I was excited to be a part of this American couple's Big Day.

Had I been able to read the future, I likely would have postponed leaving to do my duty to the students. Their return to Florida would be more of a drama than any of us anticipated. Sara Fasel recorded the excitement, disappointment, boredom and ultimate joy of those final days in her diary, starting with the night of the Bolshoi ballet when we said our goodbyes.

The ballet was wonderful and the theatre beautiful. When we got back to the hotel, I said goodbye to Mark because he is leaving tomorrow morning to go home. I wish I could go with him because I don't really like Moscow. I loved Chelyabinsk, but Moscow isn't anything special. I can't wait until we get to go home.

May 4 (Next day)
Today we went to the airport, unloaded all our stuff and then we found out a horrible thing: our plane was delayed a whole day. I was almost crying. We were all ready to see our families, and then we couldn't. Well, Pan Am sent us to a different hotel and we spent the day moping around. At dinner time, we walked to the Metro and rode to Pizza Hut (again). It tasted so good! Then we rode an electric bus to the Red Square (again). Then we rode the Metro back, but it started to rain. So we had to walk a few blocks in the rain. I went to sleep and prayed that the plane wouldn't be delayed any longer.

May 5
We went to the airport and got on the plane happily. I was so excited to come home. Once we were in the air, I tried to sleep. When I wasn't sleeping I was catching up on my journal and thinking about coming home.

When we landed in New York I was so happy because it felt like we were home, but it was also a sad time. This was where everyone split up. The Graysons went one way and David (Stone) went another to catch their planes. There were no adults with the Florida group, just the six of us students flying by ourselves, but it was a direct flight to Orlando.

We made it on our Delta flight and prayed that the time would go by fast. When we landed in Orlando, I was about to burst with happiness. It would only be a couple minutes more until I would see my family.

We walked through the hallways, and then we saw all our families. We ran to hug each other and went our own ways.

This trip was so exciting and I learned a lot about the Soviet culture. I can't wait to go back.

* * *

I had slept little the night before my own departure from Moscow, waking up every 45 minutes to check the clock to be sure I did not miss my ride to the airport. Every moment I was praying for safe travel home, that I would make all my connections and have smooth flights. Slava picked me up in the lobby at 5:00 a.m. He is an engineer and told me he earns 200 rubles ($7.40 dollars) a month. He and his wife rent an apartment for only 15 rubles a month, but spend 20 rubles on electricity and water. The state paid for the delivery of their infant daughter, but as is customary, hospital staff treated the couple "like dirt. If you want to be treated well, you have to slide something under the table," he said. Slava is working a second job, and his mother supplies free child care. Nevertheless, he feels insecure about the coming political changes.

I gave him $7.00 dollars for the ride and he remarked that it was the first time he had ever held hard currency in his hand. The dollars will translate into 189 rubles, almost a month's wages. Seven dollars--and he's an engineer!

I waited in long customs lines at the airport but got through without incident, except when I got to the check-in counter. I realized I had forgotten my declaration form. I ran the entire breadth of the airport terminal to get another one. As bad luck would have it, I faced the same customs official who had questioned me minutes before. This time, he made me open my bags, where he found the Air Force pilot hat, the official police jacket, several other hats and the semi-precious stones. He said I could not take any of these things with me. He said they were prohibited.

About then, a Delta flight attendant happened by. She took the items--all gifts from friends in Chelyabinsk--and gave them to a little lady in the airport. I stood there stunned. The sudden loss of my Siberian treasures at the hands of indifferent strangers shook me up completely. It was a harsh lesson in the perils of flying by oneself in a foreign land, learning as you go by trial and error.

Yet, as I boarded the plane and headed for home I felt an excitement beyond compare. I had prayed continually about this cultural exchange program in Siberia. In fact, I had lived my life as a prayer. And as always, God's answers far surpassed my wildest imaginations.

God had many more surprises, coincidences and outright miracles awaiting us after that trip to Chelyabinsk in 1991 than I could have grasped at the time. We were so overwhelmed by the openness of our Russian hosts and by their eagerness to hear about God, the Bible and how to follow Jesus, that we could not have comprehended the larger drama in which our cultural exchange group played a small part, and just how magnificently God's answers to prayer can surpass our wildest imaginations.

2

The Return

It was when I was on the way home from the USSR that the enormity of the promise I had made to Albert Akmalov and the other new believers to return to Chelyabinsk within the year struck me full force. And as I pondered the risks and consequences that planting a church in this city would bring, I began to worry that I had made a promise I could not keep. After all, I was just a 29-year-old youth pastor living in a small college town surrounded by orange groves in central Florida. What did I know about planting churches in Siberia?

Dr. Robert Clark, a veteran missionary to East Pakistan (now Bangladesh), was my missions professor at Warner Southern University. He often mentioned in the classroom that North Americans are known as people who travel the globe making promises that they do not keep. I didn't want to be that type of North American.

The promise that I had made to return to Chelyabinsk with a second mission team consumed all of my attention and prayer on the flights from Moscow to Orlando. How was I going to pull off another trip within the year? Would anyone want to help? What knowledge or experience in church planting could I offer to Russians?

What was I thinking?!

I know every youth pastor at one time or another has come home from a convention or mission trip and said, "That was the greatest experience ever! God really moved! You'll never believe what happened!"

But what happened in Chelyabinsk really *was* different than anything I had ever witnessed before. We had seen God dramatically intervene in the lives of people living in an important military-industrial city of the Soviet Union.

I desperately wanted to help my church back home understand how real the hunger for God was in the USSR. I wanted to enlist them for this tremendous opportunity God had given us to help satisfy that hunger. But how to do it? An axiom about effective communication kept coming to mind. "When people hear, they forget. When people see, they remember. Only when people touch, do they understand." I had experienced all three of these realities, but the people back home could only witness the first two. They had not had the opportunity to "touch" Chelyabinsk.

One thing I made sure to do before returning to Lake Wales was to pick David Stone's brain, getting pointers on how to convince Ed Nelson and the congregation at South Lake Wales Church of God that what had happened on this trip was above and beyond anything we could have imagined.

David explained that I needed to think of two or three occasions when we witnessed an authentic move of God, those moments when you blurt out, "Wow! I can't believe I am watching this happen!" David encouraged me to weave these illustrations into a narrative that communicated the Chelyabinsk story simply but powerfully.

"Get really good at telling that story over and over," he said. "Focus on what we saw God do."

"And what if they don't believe me?" I asked. "What do I do then?

David smiled. "That's not your call to make. God already knows what He is doing. Leave the results to Him."

I listened closely and pondered the events we had lived through the past two weeks, and slowly but clearly the story emerged. It went something like this.

When I first came to Lake Wales, Florida, just out of high school to attend this small Christian college, I already knew the Lord. Shortly after my arrival, God brought me into contact with people who had traveled the world, people who had a huge heart for God and were passionate about intercession. I read two books by Dick Eastman, *The Hour that Changes the World* and *No Easy Road,* and they inspired me to spend an hour every morning in prayer.

When I assumed the title "Youth Pastor," I made it a point to awaken every morning at 5:30, go to the woods and pray for one hour, asking God to use me in the lives of young people. Fasting became a regular habit. When the invitation came for us to go to the USSR, the six students and I split up the week and each took a day to pray and fast.

When we arrived at Lyceum #31 in Chelyabinsk, we dove into relationships with teachers, students and policemen, without any kind of hidden agenda. We quickly became friends, adults with adults, students with students, all doing life together.

One day, our chartered bus stopped at a small village store. Once inside, we saw with our own eyes how difficult life was for the average person. The shelves were bare; there was literally not enough food to go around. We watched as Russian teachers wept over the plight of their countrymen.

Back on the bus, I very gently asked a teacher of Russian literature named Albert Akmalov how long the situation in the Soviet Union had been like this. I expected him to say something like, "Since last October, when prices increased." But instead he said, "It's been this way since the Revolution. The only thing that is going to change our country is if we let God back in."

I knew something powerful had just happened.

David Stone and I became concerned for our students because they were going to bed very late and getting up very early. We were afraid they might fall ill, so we assembled the team in a small room to ask them to get more rest. We were not prepared for their response.

The students told us their Russian friends were constantly asking questions about God, Jesus, the Trinity, Christianity and the Bible. Conversations continued long into the night—well past bedtime--as our students did their best to give satisfactory answers. Right then, we celebrated this moving of God's Spirit with worship songs and prayers of thanksgiving.

When we left the room, our Russian friends asked, "What happens to you when you meet in that room? You always come out different than when you go in." In answer, I suggested that we gather the next morning, which was a Sunday, in the ballroom. That way, we could *show* them what happens.

Everybody came to the ballroom next day--even the four KGB policemen assigned to security--for a one-hour worship service. Stephanie Muhlenforth sang *Amazing Grace*, Shawn Brown prayed a simple prayer, another student read Philippians 2:3-11. Then David Stone told the story about his daughter's accident and how that tragedy opened a way for us to be here now.

I shared a gospel message from Romans and concluded with a statement from the 17th-century mathematician, Blaise Pascal: "Every person carries a God-shaped hole in his or her heart." We try to fill that hole with money, but money doesn't satisfy. We try to fill it with popularity, material things, or human relationships, but they don't satisfy either.

"As Christians, we believe the only thing that can fill that God-shaped hole is God himself. So at the end of our worship services, we invite persons to come forward and ask God to fill this hole."

In response to this invitation, every single student and every single teacher came down front to ask God to fill the God-shaped hole. There were lots of tears and lots of prayers. When it was over, we found that six Russian students and a teacher, Albert Akmalov, had decided to follow Jesus.

Vica Popova, the daughter of Lyceum #31 Headmaster Alexander Popov, and I left the ballroom and were walking up the stairway when we met Mr. Popov coming down. He spoke in a grave tone to his daughter and I thought to myself, "Here it comes; we just got ourselves in trouble." Vica translated into English. "Tell Mark that all my life I have been taught to think with my head. This morning I have learned that I also need to think with my heart."

Wow! Those words were definitely not what I had expected. We had just witnessed a mighty move of God.

Since we were about to leave for home, the big question on my mind was what to do to help these new believers grow in their faith. David Stone suggested that, since everyone had been given a Bible and the majority of these students and teachers were from Lyceum #31, they could meet at the school every Sunday. They could read the Bible, discuss what the passage meant and challenge one another to apply it to their lives. Albert Akmalov could lead the gathering.

I was assigned to write them letters of encouragement regularly. I also promised to return next year to help organize a church.

I rehearsed this narrative in my mind on the way home to Florida. I would tell the story over and over again to any church or youth group willing to listen. Whenever I told it, I always concluded with a plea. "I can't do this alone, will you help?" I was urgently trying to fulfill my promise to take a second team to Chelyabinsk the following year. I confess that I had no clue about how to go about planting a church there, but I trusted God to give us a plan. And over the course of telling and re-telling the story, it attracted more and more interest, and eventually a group of willing partners.

There was yet another story about Chelyabinsk that I did not yet know, a story about amazing things God had done there more than 40 years before we first set foot in the city. Twenty years would pass before I would hear this other story and learn how it was intricately woven into our own.

* * *

In July of 2011, my friend Logan Ritchhart filmed a remarkable interview in Chelyabinsk. In it, two German women, speaking Russian, tell their own story of God's amazing grace at work in Siberia.

Nelly Schule, 78, had returned to visit the city from her home in Germany, her country of residence for the past 34 years. Her reddish blond hair matches Nelly's restless energy and earnest expression. On camera, she tells her story in brisk vigorous phrases, often interrupted by the interpreter, who must remind Nelly to pause long enough for him to translate.

"I have a wonderful family," she begins. "Three married sons who, between them, have given us seven grandchildren and three great-grandchildren."

"I try to serve the Lord in every way I can."

At age 73, Gertruda Deimler is also a great-grandmother. She looks the part, with silver-gray hair and a soft, confident voice. She sits before the backdrop of lush, green trees next to Nelly and waits her turn to speak, gazing about as if expecting to see an old friend turn up. Gertruda tells her story with a twinkle in the eye and a sweet smile that breaks across her face at unexpected moments.

"For the last nine years, I have lived by myself," she begins. "I have five children, 17 grandchildren and seven great-grandchildren."

"I try to serve the Lord in every way I can."

The first time I viewed Logan's video, I was awestruck. You see, Gertruda's and Nelly's common desire to serve the Lord was forged in them in Chelyabinsk, when the two were only children.

When the Second World War broke out, families of German descent living in villages along the Volga River in Georgia and Crimea were rounded up and sent to internment camps, much like ethnic Japanese-Americans were interned in camps on the Pacific coast by the U.S. government. In Russia, however, families were divided. Officials conscripted able-bodied men into the "Labor Army" to work as virtual slaves building factories and infrastructure. Meanwhile, their wives and children were re-settled in Kazakhstan, or Siberia, or in German villages established before the war in the distant Altai Mountains.

The fathers of Nelly Schule and Gertruda Deimler were deployed with the Labor Army to the Chelyabinsk area. When the war ended, Russian authorities permitted their families to join them there.

"When we arrived, they gave our family one tiny room in the barracks in which to live," Nelly recalled. "There were six of us children in the family. I started school in Chelyabinsk and did really well. My favorite subjects were Russian and Mathematics.

During this period of separation and exile, the German women held onto their Christian faith. Sometimes they secretly shared the good news with other Germans at funerals, or while helping a family with a dying child. There were no churches. When they rejoined their husbands and fathers after the war, it meant they could not leave for any other place. These families could only live and work in Siberia. The believers continued to follow Christ in secret, under the watchful eye of the barracks commandant. Practicing any form of religion was strictly prohibited and would lead to serious trouble.

Some eventually built their own houses where German-speaking families would gather on Sundays or other days of the week. They were careful not to give these gatherings the appearance of church services. Rather they looked like several families simply sharing a common meal, or celebrating a family reunion . . . and reading the Bible and singing old German hymns as part of the festivities.

Nelly says, "My parents were believers. We could not have church so we would gather in homes, secretly in small groups. These were very difficult times for believers. When we were in school we could not tell anyone who we were and what we were doing. That was not safe.

"Even so, there were many people who wanted to come to our gatherings. There were many people who became believers, including young people.

"We didn't have Bibles for everybody. We didn't have song books. There was a woman who had a song book and she lent it to me. I copied all the songs into my school copybook by hand."

"We stayed in Chelyabinsk until 1956. All this time we were having church at home."

There is a pause in the video interview. The interpreter nods to Gertruda.

"My story is different," she begins, suddenly smiling sweetly. "Our family also joined our father, in Kopeysk (a town near Chelyabinsk) after the Second World War. But my parents were not believers. My mother came to the Lord after the death of my youngest sister.

"There was another German woman in Kopeysk who was a Christian. She shared the gospel with my mother. That is how she got saved."

"We lived in one room in a barracks that had been converted from a hospital. Each family had one tiny room, and all the doors were very close to each other. When my mother became a believer, she spread the Word very soon. None of the men were staying in the barracks at the time. That is why they did not accept the faith at first.

"However, the women who heard about Jesus from Mother became believers and started praying for their husbands and families. They also began organizing the church.

"Like Nelly, we did not have song books, so we also wrote songs by hand into our copybooks. When we sang the songs, we tried our best to memorize them.

"Later the men, one by one, started coming to the Faith. I myself became a believer at the age of 15."

The families did all they could to remain faithful. Because Bibles were so rare, some believers memorized complete passages of scripture in order to share the Word with other German-speaking friends and neighbors.

However, sharing their Christian faith in Russian with their Soviet neighbors was out of the question. In the first place, it would land them in prison. Suspected of divided loyalties, German-Russians were deprived of civil rights to an even greater degree than the average Soviet citizen. Secondly, the atrocities of Hitler's Third Reich were still fresh memories. Their Russian neighbors considered all ethnic Germans to be Fascists who had no right to speak into the lives of Soviet Socialists.

As a result, Nelly and Gertruda, their parents and siblings, shared their secret faith only with close German friends who were trustworthy. Even then, they had to be careful. They sometimes conducted baptisms, at night, in the bathtubs of private homes. Often family members present in other rooms of the home were clueless that a baptism was happening under the same roof, such was the need for secrecy.

"Our family lived in Kopeysk from 1946 to 1962, then moved to the city," Gertruda says. "There are many things that keep me connected to Chelyabinsk. The house churches we had in Kopeysk and Chelyabinsk were not very big, but we had wonderful relationships between us believers.

"By the time we all moved to Uzbekistan in 1965, there were around 70 or 80 believers in the church."

Gertruda pauses a moment. "I want to share one more case with you," she says.

"There was an elderly sister who died. All the other sisters wanted to have a Christian funeral for her, so we did."

Then she adds sweetly, with a twinkle in her eye and that unpredictable smile breaking across her face, "Afterward, all the sisters got invited to visit the KGB."

Following the death of Joseph Stalin in 1953, German-Russians were allowed to study for university degrees. Relaxed restrictions allowed evangelical preachers who had survived the war and its aftermath to travel occasionally to Chelyabinsk and Kopeysk to encourage believers and stay connected. Between 1965 and 1968, nearly all the German-Russian families from Kopeysk decided to move to Uzbekistan, where the climate was better and where they hoped to obtain more freedom. Most of them stayed there until the late 1980s, when they were allowed to leave for Germany.

The years Nelly and Gertruda lived in the Soviet Union produced fruit beyond the borders of Siberia.

"My family lived for a time in Estonia," Nelly said. "Afterward we moved back to Germany, got jobs and settled down. When the Soviet Union collapsed, the economic situation in Estonia and Russia drastically deteriorated, so we collected several tons of clothing and food and sent it on trucks to Leningrad and Estonia.

"Life was very hard at the time, especially for the elderly people. In Estonia, we were given a gymnasium where we could sort out all the clothes and other items we wanted to give out. We would invite five or six families at a time to come and choose things. Not only families from the church, but the neediest families in the neighborhood.

"When I retired, my husband and I agreed that we needed to be more diligent about helping our brothers abroad with humanitarian aid. The Lord has laid on my heart a special concern for the children, not only the children from Christian families but all children. If they start coming to church and hear the message, they might be saved.

"The owner of one store where we live donates Easter bunnies or Christmas candy three weeks after these celebrations. We collect everything and pack it up and send it to Russia or Ukraine. We have a big room in my house just for this purpose, and I spend about three days sorting out all the chocolates and candies and sweets. We place some clothes in the boxes, too.

"This gives me great joy and I praise the Lord for giving me good health and the desire to do something like this."

Gertruda added that she was also involved in humanitarian aid projects. "Since I am alone, I have a lot of free time. Our church collects a lot of clothes to send, so I am trying to help with that."

"I cannot say that I am involved very much in the work in Chelyabinsk," she concluded, "but it gives me great joy to visit here after 46 years. I will be praying for the believers here, that God will let them grow and give them strength and bless them in every way possible."

Nelly and Getruda narrated their story against the backdrop of the unmentionable hardships of war. They had endured displacement, disease, hunger and the death of loved ones. Yet they mentioned very little about that side of life in Siberia. Instead, they told about finding Jesus and sharing Him, furtively but effectively, among exiles in a strange land at a time when Jesus was considered an enemy of the people.

"Let's stay connected," Nelly says at the close of the video interview. "Let's pray for each other and pray especially for the young people. They are our future."

As I heard this, a fascinating idea began to form in my mind. Could it be that David Stone and our Florida group were part of the answer to these prayers for the young people of Chelyabinsk? The notion left me trembling with astonishment.

The astonishment has never faded. The story Nelly and Gertruda shared before the camera in 2011 remains both humbling and exciting to me. It cast an eternal perspective on our 1991 visit to Siberia. The initial American/Soviet culture exchange had generated powerful emotions. We had experienced both the exhilaration of celebrity status and the joy of seeing our witness to Christ make a genuine impact. All that attention might have led us to believe, as is natural in situations like this, that we were the first on the scene with the Good News.

The fact is, God is always way ahead of us with the Good News. He who was in Christ, reconciling the world to himself, is constantly on the move in the world, always and everywhere, preparing the soil and planting the seed, even in the stoniest of soils.

* * *

In retrospect, I realize that the whole Chelyabinsk story might not have happened had I not been serving at the South Lake Wales Church of God with Ed Nelson. Ed had assembled a talented pastoral team. Our worship leader, Steven Darr, taught Music at Warner Southern College. Ed's father H.L. Nelson, a veteran preacher and evangelist, signed on to preach now and then, visit parishioners and keep the rest of us on track. We worked together well, generating creative synergy and few interpersonal conflicts.

Actually the first thing Ed did for Vickie and me was to negotiate a raise in my wages. When I first hired on at South Lake Wales Church, it was as a temporary replacement for the previous youth pastor. I expected to be replaced within a year. I accepted a salary that was too low for full-time work, especially once we started our family and Vickie resigned her teaching job. I had to take an evening paper route to keep our heads above the financial waters.

While Ed was applying for the senior pastor post and in negotiations with the congregational leadership about staffing needs, job descriptions, salaries and such, he was already thinking about the leadership team he wanted to build. So in an interview with the church council he asked the members if they liked their youth pastor.

"Of course, we love Mark and Vickie," they enthused.

"In that case, I would like you to give Mark a $5,000 raise," Ed replied. He added, "If you all can do that, I'm convinced that Cheri and I should accept your invitation to come be your pastors."

The council agreed.

After he got me a 30 percent pay raise, it was hard for me *not* to like Ed Nelson.

Ed was an incredible preacher. It was actually fun, as well as challenging, to listen to him Sunday after Sunday. But that was only a part of his impact on us. Ed had come from a church in Fort Collins, Colorado, where he had developed a passion to train leaders. One Saturday every month he gathered all of us pastors and lay workers together for a day of disciple training. Up until then, I had seen myself as just a newly married kid without much to offer the Kingdom of God, but through that consistent disciple training, I saw that God could use me, yes, even me, at a greater level.

Two other friends at South Lake Wales would have key influence on the Chelyabinsk endeavor, although none of us knew it at the time. Former Miami building contractor George Kickasola and his wife Margaret had retired in Lake Wales. George, now in his 70s, was a genuine prayer warrior. He prayed and prayed and prayed. He saw every miracle in the Bible happen, with the exception of someone coming back from the dead. I was still finishing college when I started hanging out with George and Margaret. Every Monday night, Vickie and I hosted a prayer meeting at our house from 6:00 to 10:00 p.m., and George taught us how to pray.

I'm an early riser, which is an oxymoron for a youth pastor. Every morning, I would be up at 5:30, out the door and walking in the woods, praying. I did it year-round. Self-doubts had plagued me since age 10, when my parents divorced, and I started to wonder if anybody cared for a kid like me. Sometimes I wondered if my prayers were going any higher than the tops of the pine trees. Then came days when I looked back and realized God had answered prayers I had prayed on previous mornings. I call it, "looking over my shoulder" and seeing His hand at work.

But no matter, I got to spend a lot of time with the Lord every morning. When I saw people coming out of their houses and going to work, I would come out of the woods with a song on my heart and new ideas in my head. And then I would step into a crazy world where it seemed like everybody was always asking something of me. My greatest desire was to give them Jesus.

At some point in those early years, I realized that I had become a person who could care for kids like me, kids that were going through brokenness. So I started spending a lot of time in the schools and a lot of time in the community, loving on teenagers. Our youth ministry grew. Students came to know the Lord and I would take them on retreats and mission trips to places like Haiti or Washington, D.C. We eventually helped start the H.E.A.R.T. missionary training village, the Lake Wales Care Center and Heart to Honduras. God was at work and my mission field was very clearly defined. It was Lake Wales, Florida.

After a while, the South Lake Wales church stopped looking for a permanent youth pastor. I just stayed on, for seven and a half years. And it was during the end of that tenure that God opened up the door to Chelyabinsk.

* * *

I arrived home from the Soviet Union to an exuberantly joyful reunion with Vickie, Gina and Zach. Sunday services, officiating at the wedding for which I had come back early, and checking up on the six students who returned later took up the remainder of that busy weekend. Several days had passed before I had an opportunity to sit down with Ed Nelson and share with him The Story.

Ed heard my heart, recognizing immediately that God had done something remarkable through this group. He even said yes when I asked if he would support a return trip the following year to help Albert and the new believers form a church.

"Absolutely, I'll get behind you," was Ed's response. "We have to do this."

Ed suggested we have a talk with Don Pickett, the state youth director who had initially given his blessing for me to organize the trip. Don also caught the vision right away, and it was time for the three of us to take plans to the next level.

We realized we needed professional guidance to do this right, so Ed and Don contacted the one person they knew who could provide it: Jim Albrecht.

Since 1978, Jim and his wife Betty had been serving as missionaries in Egypt. The Albrechts were cross-cultural professionals with deep experience and training. In 1990, Jim graduated with a Doctorate in Missiology from Trinity Evangelical Divinity School in Deerfield, Illinois, a degree he earned without taking time off from foreign service.

Jim and Betty had recently accepted a new assignment with the Church of God Missionary Board as Regional Directors for Europe and the Middle East. The post had been created to enhance cooperation between European churches and their U.S. counterparts. Theirs was exactly the kind of coaching we needed to get us through the next steps in Chelyabinsk. So in June 1991, Don Pickett, Ed Nelson and I traveled to the Missionary Board headquarters in Anderson, Indiana, to meet with Jim Albrecht and ask him what we should do about the door that had opened in Siberia.

Jim listened intently as I highlighted key events and noteworthy conversations from our trip to Chelyabinsk. I disclosed the promises I had made to Alexander Popov and his staff. I recall feeling a bit awkward at this point, wondering what this veteran missionary who had long dealt with hard political realities was thinking about the mammoth venture I had undertaken with little more than youthful enthusiasm to see it through.

I ended my remarks by asking Jim to consider giving us a hand with the planning and, well, maybe think about joining the next group of Americans we were hoping to take to Chelyabinsk.

"Yes, absolutely," Jim said. "This is a great opportunity. We have to do it."

What a relief! If Jim Albrecht was in, maybe this was not such an off-the-wall idea after all.

In fact, the idea was all wrapped up with a wall. The Berlin Wall, to be exact. The single most forbidding barrier in the Iron Curtain had unexpectedly come down in October 1989. News of jubilant Germans chipping the huge concrete structure apart with ice picks and hammers generated a chain reaction among Eastern Bloc parliaments. From Hungary to Bulgaria to Czechoslovakia, national legislatures one by one peacefully dissolved Communist rule and installed democratic governments.

Jim Albrecht felt so keenly that the winds of change would open doors for the gospel that in 1990 he traveled to the Soviet Union, alone, from Cairo. When authorities at the airport asked him what he was doing in Russia, he casually replied, "Oh, just visiting. Four or five of our churches existed here in the early 1900s. I want to see how they are doing."

Airport authorities were not too inquisitive at that point. They wanted Americans to come, so they let Jim in the country. He spent most of his time in Moscow walking the streets and praying. From there he went on to visit St. Petersburg, but returned to Cairo without making contact with believers as he had hoped.

Nevertheless, the stunning changes they saw sweeping through Eastern Europe prompted Jim and Betty to keep praying. The Albrechts believed that God was about to do a new thing in that part of the world and they wanted to be in the thick of it. Instinct told Jim that the window of opportunity would be both narrow and short-lived. Success would depend on making swift, nimble moves. Taking one's time to ponder strategy and promote a carefully crafted program would not do. Bold action was the order of the day.

Okay, it was more than missionary instinct that had alerted Jim to the urgency of reaching out to the former Communist world. Christian thinkers and evangelists who understood the situation on the ground--who were actually part of the situation on the ground--were appealing to the Western church to help reach the unreached before it was too late. History was moving fast in Eastern Europe.

"The collapse of Communism, the tremendous spiritual vacuum, the hunger and search for values among the young and the intelligent across Europe is enormous," wrote Dr. Peter Kuzmic of the Biblical Theological Seminary of Yugoslavia.

"This vacuum is very quickly being filled with all kind of 'isms,' cults, philosophies, and so on, which are alien to the Christian gospel. There also is the Western humanism now. Everybody in Eastern Europe wants capitalism.

"So it is extremely important that God's people respond in a comprehensive Biblical, but also urgent way."

I confess that at that age I was too naïve to understand the import of all of this history going on around me. I just had a desire to be a part of what God was doing.

The phrase, "the opportunity of a lifetime is only available during the lifetime of the opportunity," became more clear to us than ever before. When followers of Jesus are in tune with the Holy Spirit, He offers opportunities that might not be there tomorrow. It seems Jesus had given us an opportunity to do something in Chelyabinsk, Siberia. We didn't yet know quite what that something would be, but we did understand that the time to do it was now.

* * *

The soonest we could plan a return trip to Chelyabinsk was April 1992, a full year after our first visit. We used the time with Jim Albrecht to formulate plans and objectives.

"Our purpose is to experience Russian life by visiting schools, cultural sites and interacting with Russian young people," he wrote in a report to his colleagues at the Missionary Board in Anderson. Jim then outlined a few simple goals.

-Improve the English skills of Russians by conversation, 24 hours a day for two weeks.
-Share information about life, values and ideas in the United States, and to learn from them.
-Interact with English teachers from Chelyabinsk in order to enhance their knowledge of American culture.
-Foster understanding and good will.

"We have some larger objectives, as well," he added.

-Encourage and disciple several converts from the 1991 trip.
-Witness one-on-one to Russian students and adults.
-Strengthen the believers and lay a foundation for planting a church.
-Distribute Bibles and Christian literature.
-Evangelize.

So now we had a plan as well as a timetable. Nevertheless, a year seemed like too long an interval to leave the new Russian believers on their own without Bible teaching and spiritual guidance. But of course God was in Chelyabinsk. So was Albert Akmalov.

Albert's upbringing is an interesting story in itself. His grandmother raised Albert. She was a secret believer, and although it was illegal, every day while Albert was growing up this woman would close the drapes, lock the door and pull out her Bible. Just possessing a Bible was illegal in those days, let alone reading one. Nevertheless, Albert's grandmother would crawl in bed with him, pull the sheets over their heads and read by flashlight the stories of David and Goliath, Daniel and the Hebrew children, and Jesus and his disciples. All the time she was planting seeds of faith in young Albert's heart.

Those seeds finally sprouted in those days when our youth from Florida visited Albert's city. He made a commitment to follow Jesus. The first thing that occurred to this teacher of Russian literature was to organize a Sunday school to teach the Bible to the handful of students and teachers at Lyceum #31 who had also accepted Christ. For a full year, Albert's Sunday school kept alive the faith of those new believers.

* * *

Before I took the second trip to Chelyabinsk, our family had moved from Lake Wales to Vero Beach, Florida. In the autumn of 1991 I accepted a call from the First Church of God to serve the congregation's student ministries. The move, coupled with the testimonies of the six students who undertook the first trip to Chelyabinsk, considerably broadened the recruiting pool for our second delegation. It would grow to 31 Floridians, a 500 percent increase!

We would be 18 high school students and 14 adults, including Vickie and me. Three other married couples joined us. Ed Nelson brought his wife Cheri. Randy and Arlene Portwood, elementary school teachers with a keen interest in missions, had already logged extensive travel experience in the United States and abroad. Don Pickett was now serving as Executive Secretary of the Church of God in Florida, so he accompanied his wife Earlene, who had recently retired from a career in management.

The Picketts and 68-year-old Ray Roberts, a native of Massachusetts involved in convalescent ministry and men's fellowship groups, were our most senior members. Ron Beard, Sports Information Director at Warner Southern College, Linda Fasel, a teacher in

Lake Wales and mother of Sara Fasel, and musician John Nance rounded out the adult contingent.

The ages of the students on the team ranged from 14 to 18 years. They displayed a remarkable range of interest. There were student government leaders, yearbook staff members, hospital volunteers, band and orchestra musicians, drama performers, surfers, scouts, cheerleaders, athletes and artists. We had three Future Business Leaders of America, two Future Educators and one Future Homemaker. Three were active in Fellowship of Christian Athletes. As a group, they owned 14 special achievement awards for everything from leadership and character to science and entrepreneurial skills. Four of them had been inducted into the National Honor Society and three were listed in *Who's Who in American High Schools.*

This talented troupe included Megan Newberry, Kelli Brooks, Sarah Johnson, Amanda Powderly, Ginny Walsh, Stacey Wilbraham, Monica Piper, Michele Drusell, Margie Gollehur, Heather Wolford, Dawn Womack, Jason Cole, Chris Mazzarella, Robert McGarvey, Mark Simon and Erik Warm.

Remarkably, three other members of our student group had already visited the Soviet Union in the course of their young lives. In 1990, Marc Boyer spent two and a half weeks touring the Soviet Union with his clogging team. Greg Campbell and Karis Blunden, seasoned veterans of our first trip and now 15 years old, would be returning with us to Chelyabinsk.

Jim Albrecht planned to travel from his home in Cairo and meet the group in Russia.

In all, we were 32 travelers to the former USSR in 1992. Yes, it was now the "former" USSR. On Christmas Day 1991, the Union of Soviet Socialist Republics officially dissolved itself into the several sovereign nations which had first formed the USSR in 1922. Chelyabinsk now belonged to the new Russian

Federation. It was one of several seismic shifts that were occurring in that part of the world at the time.

If space permitted and I had the records at hand, I would include journal accounts and memoirs of everybody who ventured into Siberia during this era of sweeping change, but I have lost touch with many of them. Some, like my good friend and mentor, Don Pickett, have since gone on to Glory.

When I finally got around to writing this book, I did manage to connect with an outstanding team member from 1992 who agreed to contribute. Linda Fasel wrote a thoughtful reflection on that second encounter with our new friends in the Russian Federation, and the beautiful lessons about life, love and peacemaking that they taught us.

> There are moments in our lives that become an indelible part of our being. In a heartbeat we can be transported to a time, a place, or sights, sounds, tastes, smells and profound emotions that never leave us.
>
> One such moment for me happened in April 1991. I was teaching Social Studies, Science and Math to gifted elementary students in Polk County, Florida. While driving between assignments at two different schools, I found myself pulling off the road and turning off the engine. I had stayed busy all day, trying to avoid this moment, but here it was. I knew that our teenage daughter and five other teens from central Florida at that very minute were entering the Soviet Union. My stomach churned, my heart leaped to my throat and my spirit whispered, "What have we done?"
>
> For members of my generation, the words "Soviet Union" conjured up memories of hiding under our desks to practice protecting ourselves from nuclear bombs. There were the advertisements on TV about what supplies to store in your family fallout shelter

to prepare for an atomic war. My simple prayer right at that moment in the car welled up from my whole being: "Dear Lord, keep her safe," I whispered.

I started the car, pulled back onto the highway and finished my drive, re-stating all the reasons why the Lord had prepared this particular group of teens to seize a window of opportunity and build bridges. We believed they were carrying the baton on their appointed leg of the race described in the book of Hebrews. "And let us run with perseverance the race marked out for us, fixing our eyes on Jesus, the pioneer and perfecter of faith" (*12:1b-2a, NIV*).

As I write this, I am immediately taken back to that moment. How did it happen? How did our family get involved in a work of God that at times confounded us?

Psalm 139 declares, "For You created my inmost being; You knit me together in my mother's womb. I praise You because I am fearfully and wonderfully made; your works are wonderful, I know full well" (*vss. 13-14*). Looking backward through life's experiences, I feel assured of God's unfailing providence.

The situations our family lived through before Sara's trip to Russia were God's way of preparing us to move the message further and wider into the world. We had lived in a Third World country during civil conflict. Later on, we found ourselves in England for an extended stay. We participated in work camps and youth conventions. From our children's earliest school years, their close friends were of different ethnic and religious backgrounds. Sara was naturally prepared for a cultural exchange halfway around the world. I wasn't acquainted with the lives of the other teens that went on this mission for peace, yet one thing became very clear. God was going to use the unbridled, exuberant sense of adventure these young people carried inside them to make important connections in Russia.

After the group returned home, I read Sara's journal. I was especially moved by her description of giving Russian friends their first-ever Bible and realizing the significance of passing on the Word to others. Sara and I talked through our frustration with people caught up in narrow, local events. She displayed transparent teenage emotions as she lamented their lack of a wider world view. I thanked God for the spiritual maturity that was taking hold in her life.

Her journal referenced a connection she had made to a Russian teacher who reminded her of me. The teacher even had a daughter who looked like a younger version of Sara. As Sara described her experiences with this Social Studies teacher who resembled me and my teaching style, a stirring began in me to connect with this community in Chelyabinsk through education. Two things were clear. One, God had given me teaching skills. Two, He calls us to be bridge-builders.

Even before the April 1991 trip finished, we began planning a second trip. As time passed, the focus for trip two became clear: it was to be an educational exchange and revisit to Lyceum #31.

Sara had suggested to teachers at Lyceum #31 that they write me letters that I could share with my students about details of schools and learning in another country. During the weeks and months that followed, I received several such letters.

My Social Studies classes followed the political stirrings in the USSR as the move away from Communism accelerated. Students clipped newspaper articles to learn about these events, but the letters from Chelyabinsk were a primary resource to bring a sense of personal reality to the changes taking place thousands of miles away.

Kostya, the man who had served as interpreter for Sara's group in Chelyabinsk, wrote my class describing his experience during the *coup* in August 1991.

During those eventful days, Russians congregated at their city hall buildings to compare information, share their feelings and closely watch the reactions of their leaders. Albert Akmalov and other teachers from Lyceum #31 were at City Hall when the mayor of Chelyabinsk received reliable confirmation that Communism had been dealt the death blow.

The mayor charged up several flights of stairs, climbed onto the roof and pulled the rope hand over hand to lower the Communist flag. He tore it forcefully from its grommets and, with equal swiftness, descended the stairs. In full view of all those gathered below, he crumpled the flag in his hands and, with emotions built up over a lifetime, thrust it into a trash can.

As the crowd parted, Albert said he went to the trash can and retrieved the torn and crumpled flag, not because he disagreed with the mayor, but because he thought it was a moment in history that should be remembered and shared.

When I finished recounting this story to my Social Studies students, there was an intense silence as they pondered what that moment in history meant to the citizens of Chelyabinsk.

I used the opportunity to talk about the cost of change, the important shift toward individual thinking and governance that was occurring in the USSR. I believe God gave me this opportunity to help them discover their God-given skills and begin developing them to become better doctors, lawyers, business and community leaders, and of course, teachers.

As news spread of the upcoming trip, other teachers and students became interested and were invited to take part. Arrangements were made to send official greetings from our local Superintendent of Schools to Lyceum #31.

The departure date approached and we immersed ourselves in the usual packing and repacking. I questioned Sara about what gifts to take, what to keep handy. "How cold will it be, really? And tell me more about the food." She gave me tips on souvenirs and a request to bring her a certain type of chocolate egg that I might find in Moscow.

Her most helpful recounting was the Aeroflot flight from Moscow to Chelyabinsk. That experience was a profound step back in time. Sights and sounds left indelible impressions. It took several hours on the plane and more on a bus ride to reach our destination. Deep in the Ural forest and deep into the night, we arrived to a warm, customary welcome of the bread and salt. The greeting committee looked anxiously through our group for anyone returning from the first trip. It was obvious that a loving bond had been created here.

Our activities followed the same pattern as the year before. We took meals together in the dining hall at the rest home (what we would call a retreat center), and daily excursions around the area and into Chelyabinsk. We visited the school we had heard so much about, Lyceum #31, a four-story building nestled among high-rise apartments and budding trees. The front steps were filled with smiling faces when we arrived. On the wall of a maintenance building across the driveway, someone had painted a welcome sign, "Russia + America = Peace." Teachers and staff greeted us warmly before eagerly ushering us inside.

We all connected with a student-to-student or teacher-to-teacher counterpart. We were in the classroom setting, a place of comfort connected by the curiosity and enjoyment of learning.

I got to meet the Social Studies teacher Sara wrote about in her journal, the one who looked like me. She remembered Sara, agreed that she and I looked alike, and that her daughter Olga was a younger version of Sara. Being introduced as Sara's mother instead of Sara being introduced as my daughter seemed backward. Nonetheless, my child had built a bridge and I was more than happy to be walking across it.

That morning I was asked to read to an English Literature class that Albert Akmalov taught. I chose what I consider an expressive sample of American writing, *Yurtle the Turtle,* by Dr. Seuss. Before I began the reading, I stood in front of the students and spoke one sentence in faltering, unintelligible Russian, and then switched to English.

"This educational exchange is for us a dream come true," I said. "Americans are rejoicing at the new friendship between our countries. The opportunity to exchange ideas about education is especially exciting for the teachers in our delegation.

"We would encourage the students of Lyceum #31 in the same way we encourage our own gifted students. Your exceptional abilities are a gift from God. Develop those gifts to their highest potential. Both of our countries need capable leaders and professionals as we enter the twenty-first century together."

The idea that God created us was new to many of the Russian students. One student shared with me that he had grown up content with the notion that somehow we were just all *here*. There had been no explanation of how we came into existence. To the teacher standing next to me translating the conversation into Russian, the idea of being created in God's image was not new. Albert Akmalov's grandmother used to close her window blinds at night, take her Bible from its hiding place and read to her grandson. By closing her blinds she had opened a window of opportunity. When her grandson Albert later heard the Good News from others, it rang true and bore fruit.

Our time in Chelyabinsk included a home stay. I overnighted with the same family with whom Sara had stayed the year before. Our families had a lot in common: two educator parents, a daughter and a son. My visit was the second of several visits between our families, both in Russia and the States. When asked what I would like to see or do, I expressed interest in school supplies. I collect samples wherever I travel to take back to my students. My host family graciously took me to a general store and smiled, maybe even laughed a little, as I pointed out the supplies that I wanted to purchase: paper, pencils, crayons, and modeling clay.

My friends and spiritual mentors, Don and Earlene Pickett, enjoyed an amazing home stay with a family who were community leaders in Chelyabinsk. Among other gifts, the Picketts gave the family a Bible story book. Their hosts read the entire story book in the few days before our group departed Chelyabinsk for the three-day tour of Moscow at the end of our Russia itinerary.

The family was moved, as well as puzzled, by the manner in which Jesus died. Christ's sacrifice touched them so, that they drove the 1,150 miles from Chelyabinsk to Moscow to meet up with Don and Earlene and ask for an explanation. The Picketts spent time with the family, sharing more about the deep, deep love of God, before we boarded our plane for the States.

We visited a coffee house, an art gallery, and an enchanting park with carved wooden characters mixed throughout the playground equipment. Sara had visited this park the year before, and we both remember it fondly. That evening, we gathered around a meal of garlic chicken, a special family recipe. The food was delicious and the conversation lasted deep into the evening. After the kids tired of sitting at the table and headed off to bed, our talk moved inevitably to universal concerns for the future of our children. Would they be educated? Could they make a living? Would they be safe from global conflict?

Easter Sunday arrived near the end of our time in Chelyabinsk. Back at the retreat center, one of the leaders of the group asked for use of the auditorium for a worship service. Everyone was welcome to come. Many did so.

With this service, we changed from being students and teachers to being fellow believers sharing in the saving grace of Jesus Christ.

Such was the nature of this experience in Russia. We went knowing there was an opportunity, but not knowing exactly how God might use each of us to show His love. We came away with the overwhelming realization that seldom does any of us actually start something. More often, we walk across a bridge built by others. It is they, not us, who have opened a window of opportunity for us to carry the baton forward.

* * *

I have come to realize that prayer cover was the primary reason for the significant accomplishments during our trips to Chelyabinsk. The two weeks we were in Russia, prayer warriors back home took turns to fast and pray, setting aside an entire day to intercede for our group from the time we left Florida until we returned. Linda's husband Terry headed the list of prayer volunteers. I became an enthusiastic eyewitness to what God does when His people pray.

Our second night in Chelyabinsk, the American students gathered at bedtime in the dormitory hallway for devotions. Within minutes, their Russian counterparts had surrounded them, hungry to hear and learn. The students read 1 Corinthians 13, the love chapter, and then John 3:16. They talked about how important it is to have a personal relationship with Jesus Christ. Their impromptu Bible study/prayer meeting lasted into the wee hours of the morning. I knew then we had brought 18 of the best ambassadors for Jesus Christ we could find, and that this was going to be an awesome trip.

We adults gathered in the evenings, as well. One night, a Russian teacher who had joined us said she wondered if her natural inclination to show compassion toward other human beings was actually given her by God. Don Pickett assured her that being compassionate was certainly part of how God had created us. He then took one of the Russian Bibles we had brought along and marked several scriptures about showing compassion. Grounded in the Word as he was, Don did not let any opportunity to share slip away.

Speaking of Bibles, we had come better prepared this year than last. We brought Bibles and scripture portions with us, a total of 500 pieces of Biblical literature, and gave every last one away to eager readers.

Alexander Popov was quick to tell us that Russia did not want American money or food aid, but that they wanted us to help educate their children. I found a chance to talk with Alexander privately and asked how he felt about the Sunday school that Albert Akmalov, his Russian literature teacher had started. "I am not a Christian," he responded, "but I feel God may be coming to me through you."

One day we sat in Albert's classroom at Lyceum #31 and observed him teach the lesson. He glowed as he demonstrated to one of our Florida teachers the material he used for Sunday school. Earlene Pickett was particularly moved by Albert's leadership in creating the Sunday school class. She stood and faced the young man.

"My parents were Christian pastors and were always ready to answer the call to be missionaries," she said. "That call never came."

"I feel the spirit of willingness to be faithful to God is evident in you, Albert. I want to leave a memento to encourage you to be faithful."

Earlene handed the young Christian her father's old Bible.

"I must confess that I took in a breath!" Linda Fasel said later, recalling that extraordinary moment.

"My parents have both passed into the loving arms of Jesus. I use their Bibles every day. It would take a profound urging of the Holy Spirit for me to part with their Bibles. Earlene just understood the power of a sacrificial gift."

Our admiration for the Picketts might make it sound as if they were super humans who did not struggle with the ordinary issues of transcultural travel, but they were mortal like the rest of us, as witnessed by this entry in Don's daily journal.

Up at 7:00 a.m. Good night sleep! Earlene in bed with a headache. Breakfast at 9:00: CUKES [cucumbers], liver with rice, tea, cheese curds, raisins and sugar. Needless to say, I had tea with bread.

* * *

One day we visited an English class. As part of the lesson, the students sang "Father, I Adore You" for us and quoted New Testament verses that speak of salvation--John 3:16, 14:6 and many more. Their teacher, Helen Goreva, told us that her students had entered the song in an arts festival and took first prize. They gave the 1,000-ruble prize money to a widow who needed assistance.

The staff at the retreat center quickly learned that we were Christians and asked if we would lead a Bible study for all the center's employees. A group of the kindest people I had ever met gathered in the room to learn more about Jesus and His teachings. We requested that they join us the coming Sunday for our Easter service. Most of them lived in the nearby town of Miass. They not only attended the service, but brought their families as well.

That Easter morning service would be the highlight of the trip. More than 150 people participated, including Alexander Popov and Vadim Kespikov, Chairman of Education for the municipality of Chelyabinsk. For many, it was the first time they had ever attended Christian worship. The meeting began with us learning to say "*Christos voskris*," "Christ is risen!"

Don Pickett recorded what happened in his journal. Years later, his daughter Kareen found the diary among Don's things, transcribed the passage and sent it to me. It is a moving eye-witness account of what God did that morning.

Easter service, 10:00 A.M.

Ed played on the guitar some pre-service music as people gathered. The place filled up. We sang simple songs, like "Father I Adore You" and "Jesus Loves Me." Ed prayed and then Mark spoke. [He gave] a very simple message on love, resurrection, and what it means to be a Christian.

Ed then gave a very simple invitation. The four steps in salvation: Confession. Repentance. Belief. Acceptance.

He had all those come to the front who were already Christians, then prayed a simple prayer of salvation. He asked all those who had prayed the prayer and accepted Christ and who would live for Him to come forward. Thirty-three more people came.

Ray [Roberts] almost shouted. The Spirit of God was so real. What rejoicing. They are so hungry. Several from the village [of Miass] accepted Him.

Then I was to lead communion. Wow! What an experience. I had bread from the kitchen, which was fitting. The juice was plant juice. They brought it to me in a big soup tureen, instead of a little bowl. I had them come and break the bread and dip it in the juice.

I gave the story of Jesus' last meal with the disciples, read the Scripture and prayed. Counterparts came with counterparts. What rejoicing! Tears flowed. The artist who accepted Christ came, grabbed me, hugged me and just wept.

What an experience! As I write, my soul is thrilled. It was one of the best Easter services I have ever experienced!!!

After the service, at 2:00 p.m., Ed and Jim met with the new converts for instruction.

[Don Pickett's entire journal from the 1992 trip can be found at the back of the book.]

From where Earlene Pickett sat, she could see one of the gentlemen who worked at the retreat center sitting very still as he listened to the Easter message. The service closed with an invitation to partake of the Lord's Supper. Tears began to stream down the man's face, yet he did not move. Earlene watched as Don Pickett walked up to the man and asked if he would like to partake.

The gentleman looked up at Don in surprise and asked, "Can this be for me?"

Don assured him that Christ's offering on the cross was for everyone. He walked to the front with the gentleman and the two shared communion together.

"The results were amazing to me," Jim Albrecht would later report. "I have never seen the Spirit of God at work in so many people in so many ways. There was a high degree of receptivity among the school students, their parents and friends."

We met that evening at a *banya* (Turkish bath house), to baptize 19 of the 33 people who had trusted Christ that morning.

Among the new believers were two brothers, Micsha and Picsha. Ed Nelson and Jim Albrecht conducted the baptism. When the ceremony began, Micsha was present, but Picsha was nowhere to be found. The last person to be baptized was Micsha. He edged down the steep walls into the pool. Just as Ed and Jim were about to baptize him, we heard a voice. It was Picsha, crying out at the top of his lungs in Russian, "Wait for me! Wait for me!"

The crowd parted and suddenly we saw Picsha leaping, and laughing. He jumped joyfully into the pool. The two brothers who had been born from the same womb testified to all present that they had been born again of the same Spirit. They were determined to live the life of Jesus together.

If all this were not enough, our last evening in Chelyabinsk Alexander Popov said something that knocked me off my feet. I had built a solid friendship with him, despite his insistence that he was, at heart, an atheist.

"I am a businessman and I have a proposal that we begin an Albert-Mark church fund," he said.

"You put money into it, and we put money into it, and we will use these monies to begin the church."

* * *

Linda Fasel was named Polk County, Florida, Teacher of the Year in 1992. The honor gave Linda yet more opportunities to build bridges and pass the baton. Congratulatory cards, letters and flower bouquets arrived at her house, as well as invitations to speak to civic groups. She and her husband enjoyed a relaxing mid-summer cruise that year. Linda used the award's cash prize to help defray travel costs for her mission trip to Chelyabinsk.

Fittingly, of all the tributes that the Polk Country Teacher of the Year received, two of the best came from Russia, with love.

Albert Akmalov visited the Fasel family in the autumn of 1992. After dinner, he recounted his experience during the tense days of August 1991 and the Moscow *coup* that was meant to topple democratically elected President Boris Yeltsin and return the Communist Party to power. When he had finished the part about the mayor of Chelyabinsk ripping down the Communist flag, Albert opened his bag, removed the same torn, crumpled flag that he had retrieved from the trash can at Chelyabinsk City Hall, and presented it to the Fasels.

The family was stunned by Albert's lavish gesture.

True to form, educator Linda would use the flag as an object lesson the next time she recounted Albert's story to her Social Studies class. But this time, just as she was about to do her usual teacher thing and compare the struggle for freedom between the colonists of America and the peoples of the USSR, her students silently rose to their feet in spontaneous unison. They moved as a group carefully toward the flag and, one by one, reached out and gently touched its rips and tears.

Of all the congratulatory letters that came to her house that year, one that Linda saved longest in her file of memories arrived from Lyceum #31. It was written to the entire group of Floridians who had visited Chelyabinsk. "We all want to write and say we had unforgettable time with our American friends," it began, in a quaint Russian-English dialect.

"We speak often about new friendship we have found. You are far away from Chelyabinsk, but it doesn't matter, because our hearts are with you. An invisible bridge of memories will connect our hearts.

"'Pray for me and I pray for you....' These words of farewell song are still in our mind. Listening to the tapes with your voice we recall your face and smile.

"It was so hard to leave you at the airport. On the way back, we shed so many tears and were so upset that the first days were extremely hard for us. We hope that we'll stay in touch in letters, phone calls and future meetings. We love you and will never forget you!"

The closing salutation, "With Christian love," was followed by the signatures of 22 teachers and students.

One of them wrote a personal note to Linda in the margin of the letter. The simple message expresses simply but eloquently the indelible impression that she and her fellow Floridians left on the best and brightest of Lyceum #31.

Dear Linda,
I always watched everything you did and how you did. There is something special in your movements. For me you symbolize calm sea, a bird flying freely and proud in the sky. I'll never forget you.

The note was signed by Vica Popova.

* * *

Before leaving for home, our delegation met with the Mayor, the Chairman of Economic Development, the Chairman of Education and the City Council of Chelyabinsk. We presented them with an American flag that had flown over the capitol building in Washington, D.C., proclamations from several U.S. cities, and a key to the city of Vero Beach that came with an invitation to Chelyabinsk to become sister cities. Finally we presented each of the 28 officials with a Russian Bible and asked their blessing on the new church we were helping plant in their city.

In response to our overture, Educational Chairman Vadim Kespikov asked Jim Albrecht to arrange a teacher exchange program between our two countries and to write up a proposed plan for teaching Bible in the public schools of Russia. The proposal was also to include ideas about organizing the new congregation.

"Oh yes, I will need this by tomorrow," Mr. Kespikov added.

Jim Albrecht had exactly two hours left in his schedule that day to think and pray about his teacher exchange/Bible education proposal. Not much time, considering the project was meant to serve the more than 150 schools that operated in the city of 1.5 million residents. Yet, Jim wanted to seize this opportunity and have something of substance ready for Mr. Kespikov by the next day's deadline.

He managed to find an old computer and hammer out a draft of the plan. That night, Jim, Don Pickett, Ed Nelson and I sat down to review Jim's proposal. It basically committed us and the U.S. Church of God missionary community to five promises.

1. To provide an exchange program and bring three Russian teachers to the States for studies in the Bible.

2. To send at least three teachers for a year to teach the Bible and ethics in Chelyabinsk schools.

3. To send a Bible scholar to teach an introductory survey of the Bible to Chelyabinsk teachers.

4. To provide curriculum and textbooks for Russian classrooms.

5. To open an Educational Resource Center with tools to teach Biblical ethics and morality.

The next day, Jim presented the proposal, as promised, in a two-hour meeting with Vadim Kespikov. The first question Mr. Kespikov and his associates asked was, "What do you believe?" That took some time to answer. The next question was simpler: "Will you build a church building?" Probably, we said. This was followed by, "How will you pay for any expenses incurred?" Our answer must have satisfied them, because when we finished, Mr. Kespikov said, "I approve of your proposals."

With this hurdle behind him, Jim decided it would be prudent to establish a Bible education steering committee in Chelyabinsk itself. The group consisted of the English teachers who had been our translators and Albert Akmalov. The committee commissioned Albert as group elder and commenced weekly study meetings. We left discipleship material and Bibles with them.

"We have discovered an open and ripe field in Chelyabinsk," Jim concluded in his report to the Missionary Board back in Anderson, Indiana. "The State Youth Fellowship and State Church Council of Florida are ready to back the project with finances and to help us identify and send personnel.

"There is a core group of 25 or more believers in Chelyabinsk who are being discipled. A follow-up visit will take place in September to strengthen the new believers and make plans for future development of the church.

"There will be opposition from the Russian Orthodox Church to the establishment of an evangelical church in Chelyabinsk," he predicted, with prophetic insight. Then Jim presented another insight on how to mitigate the opposition.

"My desire is to establish an indigenous church with local leadership that will take root in the Russian culture, multiply the mission to other localities and plant other churches."

Jim's strategy was pretty much in line with another missionary strategist, the apostle Paul. He once told his protégé Timothy, "The things you have heard me say in the presence of many witnesses entrust to faithful people who will also be qualified to teach others" (*2 Timothy 2:2*).

When you think about it, the ingredients for fulfilling Jesus' Great Commission--faithful men and women who are capable of teaching the gospel to other faithful men and women--has not really changed in two thousand years. That made for simple and straightforward questions we would have to answer in order to plant a healthy, growing church in Russia.

Would we find faithful men and women in Chelyabinsk?

Could we teach them what we knew to be true about God, Jesus and the Bible?

Would they pass that teaching along to other faithful men and women?

Only one way to find out.

3

Watering the Seed

Like me, Jim Albrecht did some serious thinking on the plane home from Russia about the enormity of the commitment he had just made. Unlike me, the veteran missionary had some well-formed ideas, long years of experience, and the resources of the Church of God missionary community to draw upon in order to meet that commitment.

First on his agenda was to talk with his colleagues at the Church of God Missionary Board, particularly the board president, Norm Patton. Jim knew Norm would be interested in what had happened in Chelyabinsk because he, too, had been following the sweeping changes taking place in Eastern Europe since the autumn of 1989.

Norm was conducting a planning retreat with Missionary Board staff in early November of that year in, of all places, Lake Wales, Florida. During their week of meetings, the group watched together in spellbound amazement as the TV evening news broadcast clips of the fall of the Berlin Wall. They understood this pivotal event would set off a political and social revolution that would usher in new opportunities for Christian missions. What they did not know was how the Church of God movement might play a role in the story unfolding before them.

Missionary Board leaders soon began to investigate the new opportunities. In March of 1990, Norm Patton and Board chairman Dwight Dye met Jim Albrecht and German church leader Willi Krenz in Frankfort, Germany, from where the four men embarked on an exploratory tour of East Germany, Hungary and Bulgaria. Their goal was to make contact with Church of God congregations that still existed in these nations of the Soviet Bloc and to ask how Western churches could be of help to them.

So when Jim returned from our 1992 trip to Chelyabinsk and shared with Norm and the Missionary Board staff about what was happening there, jubilation broke out in the room. The missionaries realized immediately that God was opening this door in answer to their prayers. However, as Jim went on to outline the three-part accord he had negotiated with Chelyabinsk city officials, the initial joy gave way to skepticism. The skepticism boiled down to one question: "How are we going to pay for this?"

It was a fair question. Due to a serious gap between donations and expenses, the Missionary Board had just declared a moratorium on sending new missionaries. On top of that, the mission had recently launched a campaign called "Africa in the '90s" aimed at strengthening churches on the world's largest continent. That venture would require considerable investment. How to come up with the resources necessary to organize an international teacher exchange, send Bible professors to Chelyabinsk, and provide Scriptures and study materials to the city was a question that no one present could answer.

Jim suggested that Norm travel with him to Chelyabinsk to see for himself what God was doing there. Norm agreed and the two began making plans.

The following September, Jim returned to Chelyabinsk in the company of Norm Patton, his wife Marge, and Canadian John Campbell, Chairman of the Directors of the Missionary Board. Dale Warman, an influential businessman and founder of LIVE Ministries, and his wife Marilyn joined them, representing the Church of God congregation in Vancouver, Washington. Wallentin Schule and Karl Meyer, a young Russian minister from Omsk, Siberia, accompanied the group as translators and guides.

During the seven-day visit, team members taught 30 classes to children and youth, presenting stories of the Bible, personal testimonies and Christian music. Several students received Christ as Savior. Two-hour training sessions instructed Russian teachers on topics such as "Understanding the Bible," "What the Bible is All About" and "How to Teach the Bible." Wallentin Schule and Karl Meyer made contact with the German ethnic community and laid plans for Karl to visit Chelyabinsk at two-month intervals.

Norm and Jim affixed their signatures beside Don Pickett's and mine to the "Proposal for the Educational and Biblical Training and Development Program" that we had hashed out with Chelyabinsk Education Chairmen, Vadim Kespikov. That sealed the deal, so to speak, and we were committed to following through on the plan. Jim and Norm explored possibilities for housing the Americans they hoped would soon be coming to the city to teach more courses on the Bible. In all this, the Chelyabinsk City Council affirmed their willingness to assist, even offering to pay rent for the American visitors they hoped would come.

Lastly, the team finalized plans to host a Chelyabinsk delegation in Florida for two weeks in November. Vadim Kespikov would lead the tour, which was timed to conclude at the Florida State Youth Convention in Orlando.

* * *

Although Mr. Kespikov acted as titular leader of that Russian tour group, Albert Akmalov, due to his fluency in English, did much of the leg work to organize it. By July, Albert had faxed me the names of the 11 students and six adults who would be coming to visit us, and we went to work making this a once-in-a-lifetime cultural exchange.

The plan called for meeting the group at the Russian Embassy in Washington D.C. and bringing them to Florida by bus. Once there, the Russians would tour the length and breadth of the Sunshine State, visiting schools and churches along the way. Lake Wales and Vero Beach were first-priority stopovers, of course; however, congregations in Bradenton, Sarasota, Jacksonville, Tampa, and of course, St. Petersburg, would also host the visitors. By the time they reached the State Youth Convention in Orlando on November 30, we reckoned that the Russian delegation would have met about half the Church of God population in the state.

We packed their two-week itinerary with every Floridian experience we could think of. They went snorkeling in the Keys, shopped at Dolphin Mall and wandered the Miami Zoo. Vero Beach made them honorary citizens, gave them the keys to the city and interviewed them on live TV. They played baseball at Dodgertown, visited Harbor Branch Oceanographic Institution, and toured Lake Wales' phosphate mines and citrus orchards. Since it was, after all, an educational/cultural exchange, the schedule included ample classroom time in several Florida schools and a high school football game. As is pretty much mandatory for international visitors, they spent their final two days taking in Disney World and Epcot.

I guess I'll never know who had the most fun, the Russians who were experiencing these marvels for the first time, or their hosts, who had the pleasure of showing off our homeland to dear friends who had come a long, long way to see it. I am sure about one thing. Of all the thrilling experiences in those two weeks, one of the most thrilling took place on the bus, when two of my fellow Florida youth ministers heard the voice of God. Several months would pass before the rest of us found out about it, but the couple realized immediately that He wanted them to go live in Russia one day. That day would arrive sooner than any of us anticipated.

* * *

By the time Ed Nelson returned home from Chelyabinsk in April 1992, it had become obvious to him that someone needed to go back and spend time teaching the new believers we had left behind. Furthermore, he suspected that maybe he should be that "someone." Nevertheless, he went through a spiritual tug of war when Jim Albrecht asked him, on behalf of the Church of God Missionary Board, to take three months' leave of absence from his congregation in Lake Wales and go to Siberia. Ed recalls the struggle he went through.

> There were a variety of reasons why, I think, Jim Albrecht wanted me to do this. I had known Jim since I was a boy. He pastored a church in Chicago when my dad pastored the Church of God in Joliet, Illinois. He felt I could bring my years of experience in the ministry to the scene, maybe add some *gravitas*. Also, because our congregation was instrumental in beginning the whole thing, I could build on the momentum we had helped generate. Then there was the urgency. We had just baptized some thirty students and adults, and Jim sensed an urgency to get in there and capture the moment.
>
> Nevertheless, my first reaction was, how can I possibly do this? Three months *was* three months. I

didn't think the Lake Wales church would go along with it.

"You know, there are ways we could work around that," Jim said. "I could come and talk to your congregation, encourage them, let them know how much we need you there and why we need *you* there. But go home and pray about it."

So I did.

In my attempt to discern God's will, I recognized that first I needed the full support of my wife and family. With two school-aged children at home, Cheri would not be able to make the trip with me. Would she have a problem sending me off to Siberia for three months?

"I think it's an incredible opportunity," she told me when I broached the topic. "Remember, my grandfather came from Russia. It would be neat for my husband to spend time in the land of my ancestors."

I reminded her of the political uncertainty Russia was going through at the time, just one of several risks we faced. But risk was something Cheri could handle. She was born in Lamar, Colorado, amongst hard-working, high plains ranchers who liked to rodeo. When she was two years-old, her parents answered a call to leave everything they had known and help Jim Thompson plant a church in Fort Collins. Cheri had never been taught to back away from a challenge just because it presented risk. If God wanted me to go to Siberia for three months, she said, well, I had better go. She and the kids would figure out how to get along without me.

After receiving the green light from Cheri, I went to talk to Eddie Joyner, the chairman of the church board. Even though Eddie was himself very active in missions, I did not expect him to be wild about the idea.

"Ed, you've just got to do this!" he said.

"How can we do this, Eddie?" I said. "Congregational leaders will ask questions, and rightly so, about who will do my work while I'm gone. I'm not even sure it's feasible.

"Besides, we haven't built this into the budget. We don't have the $6,000 dollars it will take to do it."

"No, we don't," Eddie said. "But Pastor, you just have to do it. God's working, and you've got to go for it!"

"There's going to be some opposition," I said. "I'm the pastor of the church, and they're paying my salary to be here. I'm not going to be here. I'll be over there."

"We can work through that," Eddie said.

With Eddie's support, we went to the Board of Elders and told them about the opportunity before us. They voted unanimously to allow me to go.

The next step was to go to the congregation and receive their "yea" or "nay." We invited Jim Albrecht to come down for a specially called business meeting. I was nervous that night. One or two leading lay persons had expressed their doubts about the wisdom of my going to Russia, so I had no idea what to expect.

But Jim masterfully explained how the cause of Christ could be moved forward in a land that had been deprived of the gospel for long years, and presented the case that I was the person God had positioned for this assignment. The congregation then enthusiastically agreed to send me to Russia, with more than a 90 percent affirmative vote. Actually, they joked, they were voting to *send* me to Siberia for the winter. Getting back home was up to me.

I had Eddie Joyner and our prayer partner, George Kickasola, to thank for this encouraging outcome. They were the guys in Lake Wales who were instrumental in making it happen.

We wanted to strike while the iron was hot, so to speak, and get back to Chelyabinsk as soon as possible. Ironically, that gave us a timetable smack in the middle of winter. I did not choose the months of January to March to go to Siberia. They chose me. It was going to be a real learning experience for everybody.

* * *

January 1993

Ron Beard knew that Siberia would be cold in winter, but he had no idea how cold, until he stepped off the airplane and picked up his suitcase. The handle cracked and then broke apart in his hand. He stared at the shards of flash-frozen plastic.

Ron had lived through plenty of cold winters growing up in Michigan, but the intervening years he had spent in Florida had thinned out his blood. "Cold" had come to mean weather too uncomfortable for sunbathing. Ron took a breath of the frozen Siberian air and realized he would probably learn a lot about serious cold over the next three months.

The suitcases in his hands contained a supply of clothing he hoped would keep him warm while in Chelyabinsk. Ron's Florida wardrobes contained few items suitable for the Siberian winter, so at Christmas he had made a quick trip home to Michigan to scrounge some appropriate garb. Ron's dad contributed several of his heavy winter coats.

Ed Nelson had asked Ron to join him for the three-month Bible-teaching assignment that Jim Albrecht had arranged with Lyceum #31. Before leaving home, the two men packed their suitcases with only absolute essentials, but still carried more pieces than the airlines allowed. The extra bags were stuffed mostly with Bibles and gifts that Church of God people in Florida were sending to Russian friends. The pair felt very much like international deliverymen. The closer they got to their destination, the more the excess baggage charges mounted.

Ron's one consolation was that he would not be taking the extra suitcases or their contents back to Florida at the end of the trip. He planned to give away everything, including his warm clothes and his dad's winter coats, to Russian friends who could put them to good use.

The luggage turned into an especially serious burden when they reached the Moscow airport. The tour host they had hired to get them through customs and deliver them safely to the domestic side of Sheremetyevo International Airport turned out to be so incompetent at the job that the pair missed their connection to Chelyabinsk. The tour guide disappeared at that point, leaving Ed and Ron to negotiate passage on another flight without an English-speaking Russian to translate.

When ticket agents finally understood where the two Americans were trying to go and that they had missed their original flight, a new problem arose. Their bags were so severely overweight the agents wanted to charge a large sum of rubles to fly them on to Chelyabinsk.

Ed had studied enough Russian in preparation for the trip that he had a pretty good idea of what they were telling him. Only problem, he had no Russian money. So he pled ignorance over and over, repeating the Russian phrase "Я не понимаю" ("I don't understand") until the agents gave up in exasperation and sent the two to Chelyabinsk with all their bags intact.

Ed and Ron arrived in the wee hours of the following morning. Most of the large welcoming delegation had gone home, leaving only Tanya Lukjanohikova and Alexander Popov waiting at the airport, both of whom were worried sick that something horrible had happened to their visitors.

Nevertheless, when Ed and Ron emerged from the arrival gate, the atmosphere, if not the air temperature, warmed up immediately. Bear hugs and kisses greeted the travelers. Warm bread and salt appeared, as per Russian protocol. Their hosts even offered formal welcome speeches, somewhat scripted but nonetheless sincere. As they left the airport for the drive into the city, conversation turned to the who, what, where and how of their three-month stay in Chelyabinsk.

Ed and Ron had come to teach Russian students and teachers a basic course in Bible-based morals and ethics. The plan was to teach every class from Kindergarten through 11th grade. Actually, Ed would be doing the Bible teaching. Ron had come along to shoot photos and video footage of the experience.

Videography was Ron's gift. During summer breaks at Warner Southern University, he had learned to make promotional videos under the tutelage of Warner professor Jim Kragel. The job gave him the itch to work in video production as a career. Chelyabinsk would offer an opportunity to sharpen his skills.

Ron's primary job while in Siberia, however, was to take care of Ed Nelson.

Mrs. Cheri Nelson herself had given Ron this assignment. Once she had granted her husband permission to return to Chelyabinsk, Cheri started taking certain measures to ensure his well-being. A major item on her list was to find a suitable traveling companion for Ed.

She settled on Ron Beard.

The Nelsons had become acquainted with Ron a few years prior, when their daughter Jennifer was a member of the vocal ensemble New Way Singers and Ron accompanied the group on tour as a chaperon. Cheri Nelson took note of Ron's easy-going, can-do personality. She knew he worked well with people and decided he could work well with her husband.

"I really liked Ron," she said. "He was just a giving, supportive type of person. I thought he would make a good coworker because we needed someone who was laid back, not as intense as Ed. That's why he had my approval.

"And frankly, I didn't see anybody else standing up to volunteer."

Once she had made her selection, Cheri told Ed to approach Ron and invite him to go to Chelyabinsk. Ron recalls the day he and Ed were dining at separate tables at Fat Boy's restaurant in South Lake Wales, and Ed stopped by his table after the meal to deliver his proposal.

"The first question I got from Ed was not, 'Would you like to travel to Russia with me?' but 'Do you have to work to go to school?' or something like that," Ron recalled.

"He meant to say that, if I were unable to earn money for college for three or four months, would it be a hardship? That was a strange question, coming just out of the blue as it did.

"But today, I understand it completely because I've come to learn the importance of not being in debt. I have seen so many couples in debt coming out of college. Their hearts are for the mission field, but they have already spent their future and will miss out.

"Ed's concern for me and my situation convinced me that I ought to give his offer serious consideration, and I did. And things worked out. When God asks you to do what He wants you to do, you can do it."

Once Ron signed on, Cheri gave him the necessary instructions. "My husband gets moody if he doesn't get to eat," she cautioned, "so be sure he eats. And remember that he is a morning person. He doesn't like to talk much at night."

Ron took her advice seriously, which resulted in the production of a detailed journal of the trip. "I wrote in that old journal every night. Once we got back to our room, there was nothing much else to do.

"And I read more books in those three months than I had in a several years, total."

The trip gave Ron an opportunity to hit his stride as a videographer. Upon returning from Russia, Ron would go on to complete a summer internship with the prestigious Los Angeles Film Study Center. After graduation from Warner, he worked several years on freelance productions for TV shows, commercials and public safety videos before landing his current job with the United States National Aeronautical and Space Administration (NASA). [Interested readers may view his stellar NASA photos, videos and podcasts at www.nasa.gov/nasaedge.]

Upon their arrival in Chelyabinsk, Ed and Ron settled into the sparsely furnished room they would share for the next 90 days. It featured two single beds, two chairs and two end tables. Familiar creature comforts were lacking. Sometimes they had heat, sometimes not. Some nights they had lights, others not. Basic commodities regularly disappeared from the grocery stores. One might be able to buy salt all week, but not on Friday. Meat was on sale Wednesdays, but not Saturdays. One had to learn when to shop, and when not.

The two men adapted to living with less and making simpler lifestyle choices. For example, they took turns walking to the bathroom down the hall to shower and change clothes. Ed, the morning person, was always up first so Ron learned to postpone his shower time in deference to his team leader. This minor kindness was one of several that helped the pair maintain a genial relationship.

As best he could, Ron followed Cheri Nelson's suggestions on how to take care of her husband. For his part, Ed did his best to take care of his coworker. Their hosts scheduled visits to several university classes. At every stop, Ed would announce in rehearsed Russian, "Ron is single and needs a Russian wife!" The appeal always triggered laughs from the teachers and giggles from the female students.

Ed made sure he and Ron practiced their Russian regularly, mostly during evening meals. That was the only hour of the day when the pair was free of official escorts and able to focus on language learning.

One of the cooks at the cafeteria named Natasha took an interest in the two Americans. She proved a valuable asset to Russian language learning. Nearly every day she would join them at their table and break into the conversation when the two men began to speak English.

"Мы не говорим по-английски здесь! (We don't speak English here!)" Natasha would declare. "Только русский. (We only speak Russian). If you want to eat, speak Russian." Ed and Ron spoke Russian, fearful they might otherwise go hungry. The two picked up more usable phrases over dinner than at any other time.

Ed made sure the duo took advantage of every opportunity to interact with Russian speakers. Once Ron developed a cold sore and Ed insisted he see a doctor who had once offered his services. The cold sore was a minor annoyance that did not require medical attention, but Ed and Ron saw it as a door that God had opened to make friends with the doctor, so why not?

Ed himself once came down with a serious chest cold and sought medical advice. The prescribed treatment was not quite the kind he was expecting.

"Sleep every night beside an open window," the doctor said. "It will help kill the germs."

Ed thought maybe the doctor was making a crude joke. Outdoor temperatures regularly dipped to 40 degrees below zero at night. In Ed's view, keeping the window open was not a prudent idea. But the doctor was serious. Ed decided to try it. To his everlasting amazement, he quickly recovered.

Despite the cold, culture shock and craving for home, or perhaps because of these things, the two men learned to work as an effective team. Ron would forever remember the moment at the end of March when they were packing their suitcases in the sparsely furnished room, preparing to return to Florida.

"Out of the blue, Ed turns to me and says that I was the best roommate he had ever had on any trip he ever made.

"I just smiled and said to myself, 'Thank you, Cheri!'"

* * *

Effective teamwork was essential to complete the assignment God had given Ed and Ron to perform during their three months in Chelyabinsk. It was a daunting assignment to be sure.

The Russian Federation's Ministry of Education had recently made a historic turnaround on long-standing animosity toward religion. Russian officials in Moscow extended an invitation to Western Christians to come teach Bible-based moral values to students and faculty in the nation's schools, the same kind of invitation that the Chelyabinsk City Council had extended to the Church of God missions community. The irony—that America's atheist rival in the Cold War was begging us to introduce Christianity to its children at a time when our own public schools were restricting or even eliminating religious speech on campus--was not lost on keen observers. Cal Thomas published a syndicated column in the April 17, 1992, *Los Angeles Times* entitled "The Bible: Welcome in Russia, discarded by American society." In it, he cited a program that had placed four million Bibles in the homes of Muscovites, all of whom claimed to be unbelievers but nevertheless wanted to read the book that had been withheld from them for seven decades.

"How sad that even unbelieving Russian officials realize they may benefit from something they were not allowed to have, while America has discarded something it had from the beginning and now chooses to ignore," Thomas commented.

All those years Communist leaders in the USSR were busy suppressing information about the spiritual realm, Russian scientists continued conducting extensive investigations into the natural world. One of the nation's foremost scientific communities was based in Chelyabinsk. The sons and daughters of some of the world's top physicists, mathematicians, chemists and engineers studied at Lyceum #31, the magnet school that would serve as academic host to Ed and Ron while on their mission to teach the Bible in the city's schools. Just another incredible irony.

Lyceum #31 Headmaster, Alexander Popov, lent enthusiastic support to the project from the start. He kept the Russian Bible in his office that we had presented to him on our first visit in 1991, and read it every day. Alexander endorsed scripture reading as an essential intellectual and academic discipline.

Ed Nelson discovered that, despite its scarcity, the Bible had aroused considerable interest in Chelyabinsk academic circles. One of his first tasks would be to figure out how to equitably distribute the five boxes of Bibles that he and Ron had brought with them in their excess baggage.

"The first question I got when I started teaching the teachers was, 'Can you get me a Bible?' They just really wanted a Bible.

"The language of these old Bibles was archaic Russian, as difficult for modern readers to understand as the English in Chaucer's *Canterbury Tales*. Versions of the Scriptures in contemporary Russian had not yet become available. Nevertheless, teachers and students were eager to have a Bible of their own.

"We taught the Bible material primarily to English classes. I spoke totally in English, the American variant, of course. They had been learning the British dialect, so they saw this as an opportunity to learn to understand American speech.

"Sometimes with the younger students, a teacher thought interpretation was necessary and she would break in and help me. But by the time students made it to the 10th grade, they were expected to understand every word I said. So, they wanted me to speak English constantly in class."

The language barrier did assert itself in an especially difficult way when it came to religious speech. Biblical words had largely disappeared from the Russian language during 70 years of atheism.

"Concepts of salvation, justification, or even the resurrection, all of those kinds of things had pretty much been scrubbed out of their language and understanding," Ed said. "They had no recollection of them.

"I would often point out to them some of the references to God and the Bible that still existed in their language. For instance, '*Subbota*', the word for 'Saturday' in Russian, is a transliteration of the word 'Sabbath.' The word used for 'Sunday' is '*Voskreseniy*' with literally means 'Resurrection Day.'

"They didn't know that. I was able to point out to them that words they used commonly were rooted in Christianity, the faith that had been torn from their country when Communism arrived."

Ed and Ron arrived at Lyceum #31 for their first class at 8:00 a.m. every day, Monday through Friday. They finished teaching at 2:30 p.m. From there the pair would go to other schools, or sometimes to prisons, sometimes to churches. They received invitations to teach Bible from the Church of the Splitters, an ancient

Orthodox denomination, and even some Muslim congregations.

The pastor of the Seventh Day Adventist church became very supportive of the teaching mission in Chelyabinsk. He had Ed and Ron over to his house for vegetarian meals, and invited them to join in Sabbath services at his church.

Baptist churches, on the other hand, extended no invitation to the pair to visit their meetings. Afraid that Glasnost would not last, they feared contact with the American visitors would leave them exposed to backlash should official atheism return.

Still, Ed and Ron rarely had an evening free. Saturday was an extra school day in Russia, so often their weekend schedule included invitations to speak in classes at various city schools.

Before leaving Florida, Ed had requested and received permission to use the *Bethel Bible Study Series* to teach an overview of the Old and New Testaments to English-speaking teachers in the city. He taught these classes every Tuesday and Thursday night for two and a half hours, trying to cram as much Bible content as possible into the three months.

Once Chelyabinsk teachers and scientists had a chance to read the Bible for themselves, they would question everything Ed said in class.

"Their minds worked in a very methodical, almost mechanistic way," he said. "'How could God ask Abraham to kill his own son? How can this be?' And 'How could the resurrection be real?'

"They had never thought about the Bible as a document written in a historical context. They were just looking at the text in sort of a theoretical way. It seemed so foreign to them."

Ed found himself going back time after time to an oft-repeated statement of the authors of the Bethel Series. "You have to think Hebrew here, not Russian." His students would invariably ask, "What do you mean by thinking in Hebrew?"

He would answer that Hebrew thought always asks a simple question, not always a scientific question, not necessarily the kind of question the scientific method asks. Always the Hebrews ask one question about their stories: "Who?" The answer is always "God."

"I would tell my students, 'You have to think with the pictorial mind of the Hebrews, and when you are trying to understand a text of Scripture, always ask the same question that they did.

"That simple question, 'Who?' seemed to help them put the Old Testament, and eventually the New Testament, into context."

As his students progressed through those Tuesday and Thursday night classes, Ed made it clear that absolutely no question was out of bounds. He was not sure all of the teachers came to the conviction that the Bible was real and true, but more than one came up to him afterward and said how much the Bible teaching had opened new horizons to them.

One man put it this way: "The Bible is a huge mansion with many rooms. And in every room there is something amazing, interesting, challenging. If you had never taught us the Bible, I would never have seen any of that."

People were hungry to hear the message. Some actually admitted, "I'm an atheist, but tell me about Jesus!" In essence they were saying, "Give me a reasonable explanation for this faith you teach, and I just might believe that there is a God and that Jesus is His son."

* * *

One of the first Russians with whom Ed Nelson struck up a friendship was a big man by the name of Vladimir Galkin. Vladimir was huge in every way. The CEO of a large mining corporation, he stood 6'4" (198 cm) tall. Robust in physique and gregarious by nature, the wealthy industrialist had become one of the most influential men in the city.

No two men could have come from more different backgrounds than Vladimir Galkin and Ed Nelson, yet they became instant friends. They spent hours together playing hockey and touring Vladimir's mining operation. Vladimir invited Ed to his home for dinner and he let him dance with his wife. He took his American friend along to the *banya* for evening baths and even hosted him one weekend at his lakeside retreat. Vladimir opened many doors for the American Bible teacher during his three months in Chelyabinsk.

Perhaps Vladimir's largest asset and the reason for his immense popularity was his huge heart. Ed learned to appreciate his Russian friend's love for life. Vladimir was a man who liked to party.

He could find a reason to party virtually any time or place. For instance, the summer following Ed's missionary assignment in Chelyabinsk, Vladimir visited the United States with a group of fellow Russians. Cheri Nelson joined the welcome party that traveled overland to Florida with the visitors. She recalled an unabashedly "Vladimir moment" while en route.

"There was some music playing on our bus and Vladimir suddenly jumps up and says, 'We dance!' He sweeps me up in his arms and we go dancing up and down the aisle.

"They are a very, um, hearty group of people."

"Aw, he probably did that because he knew you were my wife," Ed rejoined. "Because I danced with his wife when Ron and I were over there, he wanted to dance with you."

Ed suspects that Vladimir had been an outrageously horrible Communist because the man did not like boundaries. He revealed that trait rather convincingly when the Nelson's friend Doug McEvoy took Vladimir to the beach in Florida. Stepping onto the warm sand, Vladimir turned to Doug and said, "We swim!" With that, he stripped off his clothing and waded knee-deep into the water, as naked as the day he was born.

"It would have not have been quite so bad had he actually *swam*," Ed explained. "But Vladimir did not know the English word for 'wade,' so to him he was swimming. Vladimir always did things his way."

Ed's friendship with Vladimir produced one of the more alarming moments that he endured during his three months in Russia. He, Vladimir and Ron spent a relaxing evening at the *banya* with some of the important men of the city, telling stories and enjoying male bonding time. At one point, Ed reminded Vladimir of the curfew at the dormitory where he and Ron Beard were staying. "No problem!" Vladimir exclaimed.

It was, of course, not a problem for Vladimir. Rules were for other people. He lived life his way.

As the evening wore on, Ed and Ron got more and more nervous. Their curfew hour was fast approaching and the trio was still hanging out in togas at the bathhouse. Finally, Ed said, "Vladimir, we have to go! Now!"

"No problem," came the reply. "I know shortcut. We go through the park."

As it turned out, it was a problem. Unbeknownst to the two Americans, Chelyabinsk authorities had declared it illegal for citizens to enter the park after dark. Vladimir knew that, of course, but rules were for other people.

The men dressed quickly, jumped in the car and sped off through the streets of Chelyabinsk. Finally, they came to the park and the lane that would take them a straight shot to the dormitory building. They almost made it.

Suddenly two police cars with sirens blaring and lights flashing pulled Vladimir's limousine over to the curb. Four officers jumped out and surrounded the car,

Uzis pointed at the occupants. They ordered the passengers out of the car while screaming "*ruki vverkh!*" (Hands up!). They slammed the men against the limo and performed a thorough full-body search. Ed realized they were going to a Russian jail. He had seen some Russian jails. They were not pretty.

Vladimir suddenly cried out in desperation, "*Eto Amerikanskiye muzhchiny*! These are American men!" He quickly explained to the officers that Ed and Ron were the missionaries that had come to Chelyabinsk to teach the Bible.

Fortunately, nearly every one of the million and a half residents of the city had heard about the Americans, including these four policemen. That was the only thing that saved them from jail that night. In fact, had Ed and Ron been Russian, they could have been in jail for a long, long time.

Ed eventually came to realize that what drew Vladimir to him was not his knowledge of Jesus so much as his firsthand experience with capitalism. Vladimir exuded optimism about the new opportunities presented by Russia's embrace of a free-market economy. He wanted to learn everything he could about how capitalism worked in real life. Ed was Vladimir's window into this new world.

Ed was happy to share what knowledge he possessed and answer Vladimir's questions about capitalist opportunities, but as his time in Russia drew to an end, Ed realized that what he really wanted to share with Vladimir was knowledge of the greatest opportunity in the world--the gospel of Jesus Christ. To this point in their relationship, the big Russian had carefully avoided the subject. Ed believed that his friendship with Vladimir had earned him the right to share with him the one, most important thing in his life.

So, he made an appointment with the busy industrialist one Friday night at 9:00 p.m. at Vladimir's corporate office. Equipped with a *Four Spiritual Laws* tract in Russian and a trusted translator, Ed walked into the office and asked, "We have become friends, haven't we, Vladimir?"

"Certainly! You have danced with my wife. You have sat in the banya with me, you went to my retreat. *Da,* we friends."

"Then can I share with you the most important thing in my life?" Ed asked. Vladimir nodded his permission.

Ed began to share the Four Spiritual Laws. Law one, God loves us and has a wonderful plan for each of our lives. Two, when a man is separated from God by sin, he cannot experience God's love and plan. Three, Jesus Christ is God's provision for man's sin. Only through Him can a man know and experience God's plan for his life. Four, we must individually receive Jesus Christ as Savior and Lord. Then we can know and experience God's love and plan for our life. *(Bill Bright, Campus Crusade for Christ, c. 1994)*

Ed finished and looked at Vladimir. "Is this all clear to you?"

The big Russian looked back and said, "*Da.* I believe One and Four."

"Well, maybe I didn't make something clear here," Ed said carefully. "Let me try again."

Ed explained the Four Laws a second time and a light bulb seemed to go on in Vladimir's head. He said, "Good, Ed, now I understand. Now I believe One, Three and Four."

It appeared that the idea that he was a sinner was too much for Vladimir to accept. To admit that would be to admit that he was needy, deficient perhaps, and that he needed help to fully experience the life God desired for him. He was so sure of his own resources, his own self-sufficiency, Ed concluded, that to confess his spiritual poverty was simply out of the question.

Vladimir, it seemed, was content to be just three-fourths redeemed. Ed feared that this man who loved to party would miss out on the greatest Party ever.

Ed went home that night with a prayer on his lips and hope in his heart that his big Russian friend would one day fully embrace his Savior. When that time came, the two men would be not just friends, but brothers.

*   *   *

Ed did become brothers with Dimitry Spacibokov before he left Russia.

Dimitry was as different from Vladimir as two men could be. At birth, the part of his brain that operates motor skills was damaged by clumsy use of birthing tongs. Dimitry's ability to crawl, let alone stand or speak was impaired.

His parents placed him in a special boarding school for crippled children. He grew up with physically challenged children like himself, segregated from society. Through sheer tenacity of will, Dimitry taught himself to crawl, then stand, walk and talk. He even eventually taught himself the English language and became the English teacher in the boarding school where he was raised.

When Ed visited Dimitry's school in Chelyabinsk and met him for the first time, it was difficult for the American to look the young man in the eye. Dimitry's face was twisted. His arms, legs and fingers were so grotesquely bent that Ed could literally feel his pain, almost to the point that he wondered if he could endure the meeting.

Dimitry's soul was crippled, as well. Growing up in an atheist society had taught him to mock Christ all his life. However, one day Dimitry viewed Bill Bright's film about Jesus, *A Man without Equal*, and it sparked his interest. When the video ended, he hobbled up to Ed and asked, "Can I come to your classes?"

Ed gave his permission.

Dimitry made his way every Tuesday and Thursday to Ed's Bible class. He was also present on Sunday mornings at worship. Through snow and ice, with great effort, the physically challenged English teacher took advantage of every occasion to hear the gospel of Jesus.

One day, about three-fourths of the way through the New Testament overview class, Ron was interviewing Dimitry on camera for a video presentation, and casually asked him what the teachings about Jesus were doing for him.

"It is as if someone is drawing back a veil," Dimitry said, his voice quiet and clear. "I have been, well, born a second time."

Indeed, Dimitry was born again. Several weeks later, on the next-to-last Sunday before Ed and Ron ended their mission to Chelyabinsk, they baptized Dimitry as testimony that he had trusted Christ as Savior and Lord, and although his body was broken and twisted, he had been made whole in Jesus.

When Ed and Ron concluded their work in Chelyabinsk and returned to Florida, they left behind a group of 100 persons who gathered every Sunday morning in Albert Akmalov's class room at Lyceum #31 for worship and Bible study.

"This group of seekers and new believers could not yet be called a church in the strictest sense of the word," Ed said. "But it was the seed that would eventually grow into the Церковь Бога (Church of God) in Chelyabinsk, Russia.

* * *

Cheri Nelson immediately picked up on the reverse culture shock her husband experienced upon his return to Florida. "It was almost like he was a little bit angry and depressed," she said. "He came back to the fast pace, the rudeness, the overindulgence, and he felt almost guilty because of the things we had.

"We, that is, the family, had not spent three months in Russia like Ed. We had not dealt with the privations, so we were part of the problem. We could not understand where Ed was coming from."

"Understand, living in Russia in the early 1990s was a bit like living in a black and white movie from the 1930s," Ed said. "Everything was sort of dark, dingy and dreary.

"That explained why human relationships were so much more important to Russian people than to us. Relationships were all they had.

"So I came back home feeling guilty that I had all this stuff that I didn't need. I felt paralyzed in the 3,000-square-foot home that we lived in. I had entered Russian homes not any bigger than our kitchen.

"Ron and I lived out of two suitcases in that tiny room for three months and we were perfectly fine with nothing. Nothing!

"I was not a little angry, I was *very* angry. And I couldn't understand why."

Ed's gaze focused on something for a moment, a distant memory of that worldview-altering experience in the cold Siberian winter.

Then with a wry smile, he added, "Yeah, it was tough. But I got back into becoming a greedy American almost right away."

* * *

Greedy American or not, Ed had stepped into a God-given opportunity to carry the Good News to Russia at a crucial juncture in history. By doing so, he was able to speak into the lives of hundreds of Russians who yearned for something more. "Something more" meant for many of them an expected improvement in the quality of life. And life certainly did improve for most Russians, at least in terms of access to consumer goods.

In April of 2001, the Nelsons returned to Chelyabinsk with Vickie and me to lead a marriage conference and celebrate the 10-year anniversary of the church's founding. We saw a different country, a country that was becoming more like the United States and its consumer-oriented economy.

"There was color, there were billboards," Ed observed. "There was choice in the grocery stores, where there had been no choice before. There was joy, there was laughter. True, genuine laughter.

"It had changed in those 10 years, but not always for the better. Now there was pornography, all kinds of ugly stuff. Human trafficking that had been kept under control by the Communists was now out in the open."

"And divorce," Cheri said. "Before, you couldn't get a divorce. When that opened up, there were a lot of divorces that took place."

The spike in divorce was symptomatic of a devaluation of human relationships in general.

"This is one thing we both know," Cheri said. "The first time we went over there, relationships were so important. That was really all they had.

"For instance, on our 1992 trip we found out that the girl who was our interpreter, who hosted us for our homestay, was working for the KGB to make a little extra money.

"But it wasn't that she didn't like us. She loved us!

"When we went back 10 years later, we didn't sense that kind of human warmth anymore. That was the thing that I really missed."

"Yes, we organized a little reunion with some of the people I had developed such close relationships with 10 years earlier," Ed said. "But it wasn't the closeness we felt before."

"They seemed to have difficulty making time for us. 'Let me call you back,' was the standard reply to our requests for get-togethers. Old friends were now very distant.

"Our consumerism brought some positive things, but also some negative things."

Despite slick marketing messages to the contrary, comfort and convenience do not lead to spiritual well-being. The God-shaped hole in the human heart can only be filled with God.

* * *

Some months before Ed and Ron went to Russia in January 1993, a letter came unexpectedly to a member of the Vero Beach Church of God. The Russian woman who wrote it had not met Trish personally. Somehow a letter written by Trish, along with articles clipped from magazines and a photograph of Trish and her husband Al, had fallen into the hands of the letter's author, Lidia. That was enough to commence a correspondence.

Trish passed along Lidia's letter to me and I kept it in my file of memories and illustrations. I share parts of it here because Lidia simply but beautifully expresses how she and her countrymen were awakening to the possibility that God does, in fact, exist and welcomes every one of us to know Him.

July 16, 1992

Dear Trish,

Thank you very much for your wonderful letter, your picture and the copies of the news articles. I read the story "Footprints" to my students and we had a discussion. One of them asked why God helps one and does not help another in troublesome times, whether He is partial or impartial. I am not absolutely sure that I could answer their questions as well as any of you might answer, but the thing that I liked most of all was that my students were interested and took everything so seriously, in earnest. It impacts our relations, making them extremely warm and cordial.

Now that I am writing, I have your picture before me and it looks as if I really were *talking* to you. Seeing your smile, I feel you understand me and sympathize with me. Thank you! I am sure your husband Al was a charming person, sincerity and kindness flowing out of his smile, too.

It is always interesting to learn the way foreigners see us Russians. The articles you sent me give an idea of it, though rather vague. One should live with the family, not a day or two, but a week at least, to live the life of a member of the family through all the daily cares and troubles. I wish your students and adults could have seen our life from within, for what they did see was the outside of the events and aspects of life.

The delegation planning to visit Florida in November is going to be very selective. If I have come to America by this time, I hope I may join them. The most difficult thing, though, is to arrange all the things here, the official travel papers. Last week I received an invitation from the church, but it will take me a lot of time and pains to make my visit a reality. Naturally, I would like to meet the people in the churches as well as at schools. Sometimes, though, I have a haunting feeling I will never have this chance again.

The last two months have been very strenuous for my son Artyom. He was taking his final examinations at school after the numerous tests. Thank the Lord, he did well in his exams and has a chance to be admitted to the Polytechnic Institute, but we shall have to wait until the others who have to take the entrance exams have passed them.

From time to time, I come to meet a group of missionaries who have been here for three months already. They are nice young people and they speak mostly to students, so I helped them to find eager listeners for their songs and talks about Jesus and the Bible. At first, I found them interesting because we are not favored with things like that, but then I was disappointed. They spoke about what I knew already, the interpreter spoke Russian very badly (I wish there were no translation at all) and the form prevailed over the contents. But the students seemed to like them very much and to enjoy singing together.

During the visit of your delegation, we also sang with a great inspiration. I remember the moving moments of the communion in a small church at the retreat in the mountains last fall. I was surprised to see that not every one of my delegation was as greatly impressed as I. Different people reacted differently under the same situation, to the same words. I hope to get more experiences of the kind.

You may find all this very trivial, but for me any spiritual experience is very important, for it gives me a new impulse for life.

I am afraid I am not much of a letter-writer, too many emotions and very few facts. The next letter may be better, but I am not sure. . . .

I hope you feel as fine as you look in the picture. God bless you!

Sincerely yours,
  Lidia

If Lidia's spiritual awakening was common to other Russians in that brief transition period between Communism and consumerism--and I firmly believe it was--then the need to take the Good News to them was indeed urgent. We would soon find out that the window of opportunity given us to answer their questions about God and His Word was even slimmer than we had first imagined. The time granted us to share what we knew about the Way, the Truth and the Life would not last long.

In urgent times like that, you had better have a plan and stick to it, or things can go south very quickly. That is why I am so thankful that God had a plan. All we had to do now was to discover His plan and, of course, stick to it.

4

The CoMission

The apostle Paul says in Ephesians 3:20 that God "is able to do immeasurably more than all we ask or imagine, according to his power that is at work within us." Those words became very real to us as we watched God unfold His plan for Chelyabinsk. He turned one small act of obedience at the 1990 Florida Youth Convention into an extraordinary open door to a city on the other side of the world.

What happened after our second trip to Russia in 1992 came about at a rapid pace in a short time. As is His way, God was doing things behind the scenes we could never have imagined, with resources we had not even asked of Him, all the time working His immeasurable power within us. It was quite a ride.

The people involved were truly coming to understand that the opportunity of a lifetime is only available during the lifetime of the opportunity. The more we got involved, the more opportunities surfaced for us to partner with other Christians who were also seeking to make disciples of Jesus in Russia. We came to realize that the same door for effective service that was opening in Chelyabinsk was opening in cities all over Eastern Europe, including the former USSR.

* * *

In 1989, students and teachers at a school in the city of Tbilisi, Georgia, birthplace of Josef Stalin, watched the premier showing in the Soviet Union of a motion picture destined to have a powerful impact on the nation. The film was the brainchild of Bill Bright, the founder of Campus Crusade for Christ (now Cru). Bright had long dreamed of producing a "biblically accurate depiction of the life, ministry, and death of Jesus" that would reach "every nation, tribe, people and tongue, helping them see and hear the story of Jesus in a language they can understand." It was entitled simply, *JESUS.*

Bright chose his friend and coworker Paul Eshleman to produce and distribute the movie. Filming commenced in Israel in 1978, with an international cast under the direction of veteran British movie-maker John Heyman. Warner Brothers introduced the picture to the U.S. market, which opened in 1979 in 250 theatres across the country. By the time the American theatrical run of *JESUS* ended a year later, thousands of persons had come to know Christ, including some of the executives at Warner Brothers.

Box office income, along with generous donations from friends, helped Cru and Warner Brothers recoup the movie's considerable production costs. In 1980, Campus Crusade obtained exclusive distribution rights to the film, guaranteeing that future showings could be offered free to anyone, anywhere in the world. Eshleman and his team began orchestrating the most successful promotional campaign in history for a motion picture. At this writing, *JESUS* has been shown in every country of the world to roughly two-thirds of the global population. Forbes magazine ranks *JESUS as* "the most-viewed, full-length feature film in history."

Cru technicians teamed up with missionaries and linguists to dub the film's soundtrack into more than 1,500 languages, gaining entry into The Guinness Book of World Records as the "Most Translated Film" in history. Even more impressive: 530 million *JESUS* viewers have indicated a desire to know Christ.

While Paul Eshleman and his team in Tbilisi were introducing *JESUS* to Georgian students, Bill Bright was screening the movie for six hundred teachers and students a thousand miles away in the Ukraine. He and Eshleman observed the same intense reaction to the film in both venues: rapt attention, excitement at the miracles, audible gasps at the crucifixion, tears at the burial, radiant smiles at the resurrection.

"The greatest day of my life was the day I received Christ as my own personal Savior," Bright told the Ukrainian audience at the close of the film. At his request, members of the Young Pioneers Communist youth club passed out copies of the evangelistic booklet *Have You Heard of the Four Spiritual Laws?* to the audience. Bright invited those who wished to invite Jesus into their lives to raise their hands. More than half the audience did so.

Eshleman and company began working to arrange screenings of *JESUS* in 15 cities across the Soviet Union. They sent invitations to prominent political, cultural, educational and religious leaders in every place the film premiered. Civic leaders attended in overwhelming numbers, including seven of Mikhail Gorbachev's nine cabinet ministers, and key advisors to future president Boris Yeltsin. At a reception following the Moscow premier, officials in charge of the USSR educational system approached Eshleman and said, "You should show this film to our students."

That simple statement led to a meeting on January 23, 1991, between Eshleman and Eugene Kurkin, Deputy Minister of Education for the Russian Republic. The *JESUS* film's producer offered to supply every one of the country's 65,000 schools with a copy of the movie. Eshleman also outlined his vision to introduce a course on biblical ethics that would serve as a pattern to build the moral foundation of society.

"We don't know how many caverns there are in the foundation of our society after 70 years without God," Kurkin answered pensively. "You are making a very generous offer."

Kurkin mentioned that representatives from Russia's 89 school districts would be meeting in Moscow the following day to discuss the issue of church and state separation. "We will discuss your proposal and let you know," he said.

"Would you like to see the *JESUS* film at your meeting?" Juli Gusman, the Moscow distribution chief asked the deputy minister. Kurkin thought it was a great idea. So the next day, 400 Russian educators not only saw *JESUS*--most of them for the first time--they also received a personal copy of the movie's "script," the gospel of Luke.

Best of all, the assembled educators agreed to accept Paul Eshleman's proposal to teach courses on Christian Ethics and Morality. Eshleman and his associates recruited a team of American professors who introduced the curriculum to 250 Russian teachers and principals meeting the following May at the Pioneer Palace Communist youth center in the Moscow suburb of Perova. At the end of that four-day convocation, the Russian educators told their American counterparts that they should teach this curriculum and show the JESUS film to every one of Russia's 300,000 teachers, in every one of the country's Pioneer Palaces.

At the urging of Paul Eshleman and several American educators, Bruce Wilkinson, president of Walk Through the Bible Ministries, accepted an invitation to address an identical convocation held in the city of Pushkin in November 1991. The Russian teachers exuded a hunger to know God that profoundly moved the members of the leadership team. Among them were Paul Kienel, president of the Association of Christian Schools International (ASCI), and the newly appointed president of OMS (formerly, Overseas Mission Society) International, J.B. Crouse. They concluded that careful, long-term follow-up was needed, "to preserve this ripe fruit before it rots in the field."

They envisioned a plan to send teams of volunteers from the United States and other Western countries to live in Russia for one year. Working under the direction of Russian education officials, the volunteers would teach the Bible-based curriculum on Morality and Ethics in public schools and train Russian teachers to continue teaching the course on their own.

Wilkinson and his colleagues knew it would be a huge and expensive undertaking. They estimated the cost for training, sending and sustaining the hundreds of volunteers needed for the task—more than fifteen hundred in all, as it turned out--would run into the millions of dollars—more than 60 million dollars, as it turned out. The enterprise would require a lot more people and resources than Walk Through the Bible, Cru, ASCI or OMS could marshal. They would need to recruit many more Christian ministries to help--a total of 87 organizations, as it turned out.

The collaborative effort that emerged from the vision that Wilkinson, Kienel, Crouse and others saw in Pushkin soon became reality. The movement that it birthed surpassed even the wildest dreams of these three men and the many other leaders of Christian organizations who joined them in the endeavor. They gave their bold project a name expressive of both the goal they hoped it would achieve and the unprecedented cooperation it would require to succeed. They called it the CoMission.

* * *

I do not believe it was mere coincidence that the CoMission was being launched at roughly the same time Jim Albrecht, Norm Patton, Don Pickett and I were trying to figure out how to provide a Bible-based curriculum in Russian for the Chelyabinsk's 150 public schools. After all, Vadim Kespikov, Director of Education in Chelyabinsk, was just as concerned to teach his students ethics and morality as were his colleagues in Moscow. His appeal to us was identical to that which Eugene Kurkin had proposed to Paul Eshleman, which in turn inspired Bruce Wilkinson and company to form The CoMission. [You can read more about this remarkable movement in *The CoMission: The amazing story of eighty ministry groups working together to take the message of Christ's love to the Russian people.* Paul H. Johnson, editor. Chicago: Moody Publishers, 2004].

This enterprise was undertaken at a time when leaders of America's own educational system were shutting that door ever more tightly against teaching the Bible in our own schools. Under pressure from parents, lawyers, judges and civil rights activists, school administrators across our nation were taking steps to exclude religious speech--Christian speech in particular--from campus.

When a delegation of Russians came to the United States as guests of the CoMission in the fall of 1992, their visit served to highlight the irony of this historical shift. During a press conference at the ACSI national convention in Anaheim, California, Alexander Asmolov, Russia's Deputy Minister of Education, explained his country's keen interest in Christianity and the Bible.

"For 75 years we were in the desert of Communism," Asmolov said. "This philosophy resulted in tragic things for the souls of our people. It is a miracle that the Christianity of the United States is going to help its brothers in Russia."

One member of the press asked why Russia was accepting help from evangelical Christians and not from other religious confessions represented in the United States. Asmolov responded, "When a person is under a waterfall drowning, and someone reaches a hand out to save him, he doesn't ask whose hand it is. He just takes it.

"The CoMission was the first to reach out a hand to help us in teaching morals and ethics. So we have taken that hand."
[Quoted in "Coached by Americans, Ex-Soviet Schools Teaching Christian Ethics," by George W. Cornell, Associated Press Religion Writer. Reproduced here from the *Press Journal*, Vero Beach, Florida. June 26, 1993.]

Our friends in the Chelyabinsk Ministry of Education were asking the Church of God missions community for a Bible-based curriculum identical to the one that Wilkinson, Kienel and Eshleman were developing. Jim Albrecht, Norm Patton, Ed Nelson and I had devised a proposal to address their request which was similar to the CoMission plan. However, at this point in time, we were completely ignorant of the CoMission and the excellent Christian Ethics and Morality course it was developing. But all that would soon change. God, remember, had a plan.

* * *

Jim Albrecht attended a conference in Cincinnati, Ohio, convened to explore doors opening to the gospel in the Muslim world, a topic of intense interest to the long-time missionary to Egypt. There he learned about plans in the works to launch the CoMission. Almost immediately, Jim realized that this was the answer to Vadim Kespikov's plea for a Bible-based course on Ethics and Morality in Chelyabinsk.

Jim also realized he needed to talk with Paul Eshleman, so in early December 1992, he flew to

Laguna Beach, California, to meet with Eshleman, CoMission consultant Jaan Heinmetz, and the Director of the USA Resource Team, John Klein. Jim had asked for the meeting to learn more about CoMission. He realized during the discussion that Eshleman and his associates had come to the meeting to learn more about the Church of God. They asked Jim pointed questions about the beliefs and activities of our faith community. It was a vetting process, actually, to determine if the Church of God qualified to be a CoMission partner.

The meeting convinced both parties to form a partnership. In fact, when Paul Eshleman learned that Ed Nelson and Ron Beard planned to be in Chelyabinsk for three months teaching Bible classes, he asked if Ed would be willing to field test the CoMission curriculum. Eshleman realized that Chelyabinsk represented an ideal laboratory. If the curriculum succeeded among the elite intellectuals of that city, it would succeed anywhere.

Eshleman also told Jim about a conference coming up the following month in Phoenix, Arizona, aimed at introducing CoMission to U.S. mission leaders. "It would be good if you could come to Phoenix and represent your mission," he said.

Years later, Jim wrote a brief synopsis of what he saw happening through these providential connections.

God opened the door in Russia after 70 years of near closure to Western influence and Christianity. This began fermenting some years before but exploded in November of 1989. It was almost an avalanche of openness to the world never seen before in Russia.

There was a great hunger in the Russian soul for freedom of expression, freedom of religion, and freedom to know foreigners, especially Americans.

The Church in the United States was mentally and spiritually ready for this open door. Prayers for the people of Russia had been offered for all the years of Communistic [sic] domination. We were ready to share the Good News at this strategic time.

There was a newfound excitement at the possibilities of reclaiming Christianity in Russia . . . of sharing the gospel with a spiritually starved nation. There was a realization that this was a window of time with perhaps a five-year span of opportunity. It was act now while the door is open.

A bold, new plan and strategy [had emerged] that was inter-denominational and international. The leaders of the CoMission were all full-time directors of some of the largest Christian ministries in the world. They gave freely of their time and energy to see this project succeed. There was a sense of awe that God was working far beyond what we could ask or think.

-James A. Albrecht, January 16, 2008

* * *

Following his September 1992, visit to Chelyabinsk with Norm Patton and other Church of God leaders, Jim had another key encounter: a meeting of Missionary Board Directors in Portland, Oregon. There he presented the film "Candle in the Dark," an impassioned plea to share the gospel in Russia. The Board members expressed interest in Russia, but reminded Jim that, after all, there were urgent needs all over the world. Africa, in particular, was on the Missionary Board's radar as a priority field. The Board had recently launched "Africa in the 90s," a campaign designed to generate funding and recruit personnel for missions to the world's largest continent.

That discussion convinced Jim Albrecht that, much as he wanted to accept Paul Eshleman's invitation to the CoMission meeting in Phoenix, he knew that Norm Patton, the Missionary Board president, should be the one to go. Norm was the key opinion leader in the organization. If he caught the vision of CoMission, he would be able to convince the rest of the missionary community to get behind it.

God nudged Norm closer toward the CoMission. J.B. Crouse, recently returned from the Pushkin educators convocation, phoned Norm one day to talk about the exciting developments in Russia. "Could we meet to discuss this opportunity?" Crouse asked, "Perhaps over lunch at the Cracker Barrel?"

Norm accepted and Jim Albrecht went along, to listen. He noted the excitement that J.B. Crouse exuded as he talked of the openness to the gospel in Russia and laid out the CoMission plan. J.B. then invited, or better said, *exhorted* Norm to attend the Phoenix conference.

"It will include mission executives from many organizations," Crouse urged. "You really need to be there."

Norm thought it over.

"Tell you what," he said. "I have a trip to Africa scheduled at the same time this conference is happening. But I don't have my visa yet.

"So if my visa doesn't come through in time for the Africa trip, I will go to Phoenix."

Norm's visa did not arrive, so he went to Phoenix, alone. Jim trusted Norm to make up his own mind, for his own reasons, about the CoMission.

Instead of accompanying Norm to Phoenix in January 1993, Jim Albrecht made a third visit to Chelyabinsk with Ed Nelson and Ron Beard. As those two were launching their teaching mission at Lyceum #31, Jim sat down with Vadim Kespikov to present the CoMission curriculum and secure the Education Minister's approval.

I don't think it mere coincidence that, at nearly the same moment in time, Norm Patton was being introduced to the CoMission vision in Phoenix. Norm later described the intense inner struggle he experienced at that gathering.

Along with several hundred other mission leaders and pastors, I was moved during the three-day meeting by what God could do through us if we were obedient to Him. I felt strongly that God was telling me that we should be a part of this great opportunity. Nevertheless, it would demand a huge step of faith.

At the closing service, Bruce [Wilkinson] asked for each organization to write on a blackboard the number of persons they would commit to send to Russia to teach Bible in the school for a one-year assignment. Campus Crusade for Christ, Navigators, and others put large numbers on the board. Some churches also made smaller commitments.

I struggled, because intellectually I knew the Missionary Board had no resources to send anyone. Our organization had just announced a moratorium on sending new missionaries, in fact, because we were roughly one million dollars in debt. Operations were being carried out in deficit spending.

We had just approved a decade-long commitment to Africa, as well, and several financial requests were coming in from that continent. When the Berlin wall came down, the staff wanted to be involved in Russia, but we had no money. All of the above was going through my mind in that meeting.

I was arguing with the Lord about our finances, thinking surely He doesn't understand our situation. I proceeded to inform Him of that which He apparently did not know. After a few minutes struggle, I sensed a strong presence say, "Are you going to obey me or not?"

I went to the board and wrote the number "30," not knowing how in the world we could send that many CoMission teachers. As I walked back to my seat, I sensed the Devil say, "That is the dumbest thing you have ever done!" I thought for a moment that he might be right. But God said, "Do it!"

At that time, all money requested for missions had to go through the [World Service] budget committee and approved by the national General Assembly. A request for funding for the CoMission endeavor likely would never have navigated that kind of scrutiny. I even thought I would be called on the carpet by World Service and maybe fired because the Missionary Board had not approved this decision. These funds would have to be raised outside the regular budget, and that was a no-no.

But apparently God approved. I was never questioned by the World Service staff or anyone else about the cost of what I was committing us to do.

When I returned to the office and told the staff what I had done, they were somewhat shocked. Nevertheless, all of them firmly stated that if that was what God told me to do, they would go all out to help make it happen.

* * *

When the CoMission idea first surfaced, Bob Edwards and his wife Jan were serving as the Missionary Board's Regional Coordinators for Africa, the continent that could be most adversely affected by the pledge Norm Patton had just made in Phoenix. Bob was in the United States for a bi-annual meeting of the RCs, so he received the news along with the rest of the Missionary Board staff.

Norm Patton reported that he had just attended a fascinating interdenominational meeting headed by Bruce Wilkinson. He paused, weighing his words, then said something like, "The meeting concerned the coming together of evangelical churches to do an incredible mission in Russia."

"At the end of that meeting, Wilkinson asked us leaders to come forward and declare the number of short-term missionaries we would help send to Russia to teach morality in the schools. When it came time for me to stand, I did so and pledged to send 30 SAMs (Special Assignment Missionaries) over the next five years."

We looked around the room at each other, trying to comprehend what he had just said, while quickly making the calculations in our heads of the dollars and personnel issues. I think the two words that were spoken were, "exciting" and "impossible."

At first I dismissed the whole idea, thinking that this would never happen. Anyway it wasn't happening in my region, Africa. The Missionary Board had just proclaimed the decade of "Africa in the 90s." This CoMission was someone else's issue, even though it might eat into the new focus of Africa.

Our meeting ended and I returned to Nairobi. And then it started to happen. The response from the U.S. church was astounding. Teams of "CoMissioners" were drawn together, prepared and sent. Reports began to come back about the dramatic results that were taking place and change that was happening. Our volunteers were training Russian teachers in biblical principles of Christian morality that they, in turn, taught their students. New believers had planted a church. They were even reaching out to children in local orphanages. It seemed almost too good to be true.

I remember well a number of conversations between Jan and me about what was taking place in Russia. These usually happened at the kitchen table in Nairobi, after the kids had gone to bed. More than once the words, "Wouldn't you love to be a part of this?" were spoken during those late night talks. We prayed about asking the Missionary Board to give us a two-year leave of absence from Africa to join one of the CoMission teams being sent to Russia.

But the timing was all wrong. We were responsible for directing the "Africa in the 90s" emphasis. Although the longing continued in our hearts to join this frontline ministry in Chelyabinsk, we knew that God was also doing a great work throughout Africa, so we prayed for the teams that were going and for Russians to respond to their teaching.

Some years later, Bob and Jan Edwards would replace Jim and Betty Albrecht as Regional Coordinators for Europe and the Middle East. The Edwards moved to Germany and, during their years in ministry there, connected with the Russian churches that had been planted through the CoMission. That gave them the opportunity, finally, to meet and form friendships with people for whom they had faithfully prayed while in Africa, the same people they had asked God to lead out of the darkness of atheism and into the light of Jesus.

Some years after that, Bob Edwards would replace Norm Patton as director of what had become Global Missions of the Church of God. Was this simply coincidence or was it, as I suspect, part of the Plan?

* * *

Norm Patton had garnered unconditional support for the CoMission among his colleagues at the Missionary Board in Anderson, but now he faced a larger test: to convince the rank and file leaders of the Church of God Movement to promote the plan in their local churches. They would be the ones who would actually recruit qualified volunteers and gather the financial resources necessary to send them to Chelyabinsk for a year.

Norm asked Dr. Ed Foggs, Executive Director of the Church of God General Assembly, to grant him a spot on the agenda of the G.A.'s June 1993 meeting. Foggs agreed, and Norm had 15 minutes to present the CoMission plan. He showed a short promotional video, told the delegates of his pledge to send 30 volunteers, and asked the assembled pastors to help find persons willing to give a year of their life to go to Chelyabinsk and teach the Bible in the public schools.

"They will have to raise their own funds to do it," he added. "About $22,000 per person."

The 15 minutes were up, but it was enough to spark what would become one of the most successful outreach initiatives in the history of Church of God missions. The response to Norm Patton's appeal for volunteers exceeded everyone's expectations, indeed it exceeded our wildest dreams.

Later that year at a second CoMission meeting in Orlando, Florida, Norm was present to hear a second appeal from Bruce Wilkinson for CoMission volunteers. Norm pledged to recruit and send 20 additional CoMission volunteers, making a total of 50 over the next five years.

Among the 50 would be 10 volunteers from Lake Wales, Florida. That was the number that Ed Nelson, who also attended the Orlando meeting, pledged to recruit.

The initial enthusiasm perhaps masked the fact that the CoMission was an enormous and costly venture. As Regional Coordinator for Europe, Russia and the Middle East, it would become Jim Albrecht's task to prepare, send and oversee the CoMission volunteers. Jim relished the assignment. "Norm was good at delegating," he said later. "I knew I would have all the freedom I needed to do this."

Jim counted it a privilege to represent the Church of God Missionary Board at Executive Committee meetings of the CoMission. "We met to plan, pray, strategize and cooperate to get the job done," he recalled. "There was a deep spiritual tone to all of these meetings.

"From 1993 to 1995, I attended the two-week, pre-field training sessions along with each team of 10 people sent out by the Church of God. I then traveled with them to Russia to help get them settled in apartments, and introduce them to the Department of Education and other government offices in Chelyabinsk.

"And then it was an especially enjoyable time to meet them months later in Switzerland for their mid-term break."

Donors typically sent their financial pledges for CoMission volunteers to the Missionary Board in monthly installments. This obliged Jim to make periodic trips to Chelyabinsk to provide support to the teams, in the most literal sense.

"Every three months, I delivered their salaries and operating funds by hand. On each trip I carried 50 thousand dollars in cash, strapped to my torso.

"It was risky, of course, but we felt we had to do it that way."

The Russian banking system was not yet trustworthy, having recently come online to process international wire transfers. After several trips, all of them cash-strapped, you might say, Jim decided it was time to give the struggling Russian banking system a shot at transferring CoMission funds. So the accounting office in Anderson arranged a wire transfer as per the usual protocols. The U.S. bank sent the funds as per international standards, and the money . . . disappeared without a trace. Nobody in the entire Russian banking system could find it. It was gone, never to reach the team in Chelyabinsk.

Jim had no choice but to arrange yet another trip to Siberia, this time with urgent speed, carrying the usual 50 thousand dollars under his travel clothes.

Despite the constant challenges and occasional losses, the CoMission effort succeeded, wildly in fact.

"They were the best years I spent in missions, in addition to the 13 years we spent in Egypt," Jim said.

By the time the final Church of God CoMission team deployed in 1996, Norm Patton's pledge had been reached. The Missionary Board supplied 48 short-term and two career missionaries to the CoMission effort. The volunteers served in Chelyabinsk and Miass, a city of 200 thousand people sixty miles away.

By the end of the five-year CoMission project, Church of God donors had invested three-quarters of a million dollars in the five teams of volunteers. Every bill was paid, every missionary funded, every traveler safely returned home. The total cost to the Church of God Missionary Board was exactly zero.

"All of this says to me that when God is in our plans, we need to make them big," Jim Albrecht said. "The CoMission initiative was a significant affirmation that God accomplishes what is humanly impossible when his servants are obedient."

Schools all over Russia would soon be introduced to the CoMission curriculum. From 1992 to 1997, approximately 2,500 volunteer teachers would deploy to nearly every major city of the Russian Commonwealth of Independent States. The CoMission's ethics and morality curriculum, based on the Ten Commandments and Jesus' teachings, would influence the lives of 10 million Russian students, thousands of whom would decide to follow Christ.

God had the Plan. You could say that He had a God-sized plan that looked impossible to achieve, at the outset. But as always happens with God-sized plans, God kept His promises.

* * *

The 50 CoMissioners that the Church of God Missionary Board sent to Russia were, in the true sense of the word, everyday heroes. They came from all walks of life: pastors, business executives, secretaries, social workers, missionaries, technicians, homemakers and, of course, teachers. Many were retired, others recent graduates from college. They represented 15 states of the U.S.A. and one province (Manitoba) of Canada. They hailed from cities and small towns on both the Atlantic and Pacific coasts, and nearly everywhere in between. Washington, Florida and Ohio topped the list of most volunteers sent, but the hundreds of prayer warriors and donors scattered around the continent supported their efforts.

Before going to Siberia, many of the CoMissioners had traveled overseas at one time or another. Several were veterans of short-term mission teams, others had even resided in foreign countries. Nevertheless, I think it safe to say that none of them had ever lived through an experience quite like the one awaiting them in 1990s Russia. They would encounter unrelenting cold and scarcity, and occasional fear and anguish. They would make their share of sacrifices and blunders, and many new friends. Some would be forced to return early due to illness or injury, others would decide to stay longer than their initial one-year commitment. All would leave an indelible legacy of friendship and faith. As they worked to achieve the lofty goals of the CoMission, these everyday heroes became, in every sense, heroes every day.

* * *

Charles and Bernell Sandlin, originally from Arkansas and pastors in Claremore, Oklahoma, were some of the first in line to volunteer for CoMission. Jim Albrecht and Norm Patton chose them to be part of the first team of Bible teachers headed for Chelyabinsk.

The Sandlins had three clear-cut qualifications for the job: they were veteran pastors, had spent much of their adult lives in Oklahoma, and had recently celebrated their 40th wedding anniversary. Anyone who had survived the Dust Bowl, a long career in church leadership and 40 years of marriage could be counted on to shepherd a diverse group of Americans to and from Russia without mishap. And they did.

Eileen Clay, Bill and Cindy Bridgeman, Chris and Jeanette Groeber, Carol Naugher and Connie Callos joined the Sandlins for the CoMission's first year in Chelyabinsk. Each one had made considerable sacrifices to go to Siberia. All of them left jobs and family behind, two sold their homes. The Sandlins actually put their long-awaited retirement on hold. The team embodied Jesus' challenge to "deny yourself, take up your cross and follow me."

While in Russia, the Sandlins wrote home regularly to friends in Oklahoma. Many of their letters were subsequently published in the *Claremore Progress* newspaper. Here are excerpts.

January 24, 1994

Dear Claremore friends, we are waiting to board a plane for Moscow.

This is the time for which we have planned, prayed and prepared for nearly a year. We were told the past 10 days would be like a "boot camp." It has been! Very intense training in the curriculum materials, Russian history, culture and language.

There were many times of inspiration and encouragement with speakers such as Bruce Wilkinson of Walk Through the Bible. Dr. Olga Polykovskaya, Assistant Deputy Minister of Education, was with us for several sessions and our team had lunch with her one day. This was a special time for us to gain from her brilliant mind and wonderful Christian spirit.

The commissioning service Tuesday evening was outstanding. The 156 men and women, ages 20 to 81, plus children of some, were challenged by Bruce Wilkinson, Paul Eshleman and Dr. Polykovskaya.

The first six weeks [in Russia] we will be spending most of the time getting acclimated and becoming involved in their Christian Culture Centers. These centers are the creation of Dr. Polykovskaya. We are fortunate there is one in Chelyabinsk. They are for extra-curricular activities such as crafts, arts, music and Bible study.

March 15, 1994
Dear Ones, we are in our apartment, still have much redecorating to do, wallpapering, painting, and floor covering in the living and bath room. It was furnished except for a bed and washing machine.

The snow and ice are melting, so there's lots of water in the streets that freezes overnight, so makes walking difficult in spots. Charles feels as though he has grown a double, as I [Bernell] hang onto his arm everywhere we go.

We are finishing up showings of the *JESUS* video this week. Each teacher has wanted to get involved, so we've had about three times as many students as we expected. (Praise the Lord!) We added three Monday classes to our teaching schedule, and now have a total of nine for the week. We lost the fourth and fifth graders as they were moved to another school. They were so interested. We are hoping to work with them in the fall.

Our English-speaking friends are anxious to take us to theaters and see that we are entertained. A group of us went to the ballet "Swan Lake" on Saturday evening and were taken backstage to meet the star performers. Tonight we are going to see Agatha Christie's "Mousetrap."

Pray that this will all bear fruit for the Lord. [Our Russian friends] have to want to know Him, and know why they should, before they can accept Him with a sincere heart. Many have the idea that people are turning to God because it is "fashionable."

March 22, 1994

We are in Moscow, had a more pleasant train ride this time. Took 36 hours instead of the 42 in January. We want to make the trip by train again in June in order to see the countryside green, rather than white.

We visited the home of a biology teacher last week. She also has certification as a nurse and is a delight to be around. Her husband is an engineer and apparently took off work that day to cook. We found a lot in common to discuss, through an interpreter. She took our blood pressure and thought Charles' was too low, but it was usual for him.

They are a lovely couple and we look forward to more association with them. He wants to teach Charles some of his cooking secrets and there are indications that Charles can help him with his manufacturing business. Those years of work in the aircraft industry may prove helpful even after all these years. Their son is in the Atlanta area on student exchange. Their son is a Christian, so I'm sure he will be a great influence when he returns.

May 26, 1994

Dear Ones, we will be going to Switzerland in June for mid-term break and look forward to receiving mail again as our supervisor will meet us there.

We spent a week in a "town" with a population of 100 thousand on the Kazakhstan border. We were actually in a suburb, 10 kilometers from the center of Troitsk. It was probably our best week since being in Russia. We taught 18 classes of students from fifth thru 11th grades, had a question and answer time with a large group of students (volunteer, after-school hours), showed the *JESUS* film to about 75 and helped with the regional English Olympiad. All of this happened in four-and-a-half days.

Their interest was challenging. We had students from six to 18 years of age voluntarily tell us of their faith. The mother of a 6-year-old sat in on one of our classes. She said that some time ago her daughter came to belief in God on her own. Pray for this family, especially the mother that she may come to faith through reading the Word.

A real prayer concern is for nurture. There are two Orthodox churches in town, no others. We went to church Sunday morning with four students. We asked the young people to explain the ritual to us, and they told us they did not understand the service because it was in a language they do not use today. Both churches in Troitsk were used as museums from the 1930s until three years ago. Restoration work on them is not yet complete.

May 29, 1994
Regular classes at school have ceased for the summer, but we will have one class a week during June and July. This will be for those students who want to come. We will be meeting on Tuesday mornings, so be in prayer for us Monday night your time.

Two college students we met in Troitsk visited us the past week. Our English is the main attraction, but so be it. The usual question, "How come you came to Russia?" gives us the opportunity to witness to God's love through Jesus.

The city is beautiful with springtime. Lilacs, mock orange, mountain ash and plums are blooming in abundance. People are spending their spare time in their gardens around the edge of the city.

We do get homesick occasionally. The main problem is not being able to pick up the phone when we want to call. The expense is not the only factor. I called Ann last night and it took six tries before I could get Moscow on the line! [Our grandson] Jared is nine months old today. Ann and Jeff say he is standing up alone and talking some, mainly, "Hi, Daddy and Momma."

Hoping to hear from you.

August, 1994

Dear Partners, that word "partner" means more to us than ever. We are so grateful for your part in this tremendous ministry. We are depending upon your intercession for the third- and fourth-year students at the Pedagogical Institute, where we will be teaching this fall. This is the most respected institute in this region and gives us a great opportunity to influence teachers of the future to use the Bible in the classroom.

October, 1994

Greetings from the other side of the world, Siberia.

We have spent over nine months doing many adventurous things in CoMission work. We would be happy to share our experiences with anyone at any time, to the point of boring you. There have been highs and lows, enough to make us know this was the right thing for us to do at this time in our lives. Even though we are past our prime, we find that God is able to use us.

It has been a great joy to distribute Russian language New Testaments to students. Some tell us it is their first ever copy. One boy received his and within a few weeks was making statements and asking questions that indicated he had read it through entirely. He was in a group of eighth graders who compiled a list of 26 characteristics of Jesus Christ. The depth of their perception is beyond words.

You can understand why we are excited about the chance to teach in the Pedagogical (teacher training) Institute. It has seven faculties that train teachers, from Athletics to Philosophy. We are in the English Language faculty, which has 23 lecturers. This is a wonderful opportunity to train future teachers in Biblical principles. Long after we are gone, and after the agreement with the Russian Ministry of Education is completed, these teachers will still be in the classroom.

It is hard to find words to adequately describe the personality of these dear Russian people. The things we have been told through the years, in most cases, are totally wrong. They are very open to us, very generous with themselves and their possessions.

In about a month we will return to the USA. We will be leaving many friends here but returning to family and friends there. We know there will be some trauma in both experiences but look forward to the opportunity of serving once again in our homeland.

Our love to all,
Bernell and Charles

* * *

Eileen Clay worked on the Missionary Board staff in Anderson from 1981 to 1996. Like all unsung heroes in the home office who work hard to send missionaries to the field and keep them there, Eileen longed to one day take her turn out on the "front lines."

That day came in September 1993 when Eileen and her co-workers viewed a video entitled "The Red Door" during Wednesday morning staff devotions. "The faces of the little Russian children just seemed to call to me, 'Come and tell us about Jesus!'" she said.

"I returned to my office and tried unsuccessfully to shut those precious faces from my mind. Finally, I said, 'Lord, if you are calling me to Russia, I ask three things. One, an approved leave-of-absence (I loved my job!). Two, another tenant to sublet my apartment and three, my 93-year-old mother's approval of the decision.'

"Here's how He answered. One, the Missionary Board enthusiastically granted the leave-of-absence. Two, a young seminary couple rented my apartment, after my landlords had agreed to let it sit empty, rent free, until my return. Three, Mother not only gave me her blessing, but also the first $300 toward my support.

"When God calls, He prepares the way. In three months' time, He supplied me with $21,000 in finances and enough Russian to barter at the street markets in Chelyabinsk. As I boarded the plane for pre-field training at Fort Mill, South Carolina, I was excited to see what amazing experiences awaited me in Russia."

October 20, 1994

Dear friends and family,

"For a great and effective door has opened to me, and there are many adversaries," *1 Corinthians 16:9*.

As I spent time with the Lord recently, this scripture was impressed very much upon my mind. I truly believe Russia is one of the greatest and most effective doors ever opened to me, and I can honestly say that there are many adversaries. There are times when I feel as if I am facing the enemy on the front line of the battle field. I am reminded that my Captain is Jesus Christ. In Him, I am victorious!

A teacher at one of our schools is a psychologist who does not have regular classes with students. The director gave her 10 hours a week to teach the Christian Ethics and Morality curriculum to more than 250 students. We were elated. Recently the assistant principal began giving her problems because of her change to classroom teaching. It has caused much turmoil and stress among the teachers, and we spent time in prayer asking God to keep the door open for her to share about Jesus.

My year in Russia is nearing an end and I have had to really examine my heart to see if I am obeying scripture. There are many needs all around and I am well aware that I cannot meet all of them, but am I doing my best? That is a soul-searching question.

God has brought people to us seeking to know about Him. One woman poured out her questions with great excitement. Could she know Jesus personally? Could she really talk to Him and have Him answer her? Who was Jesus talking about when He said 'love your neighbor'? Was God angry at her for asking so many questions? On and on. What a delight to give her a Bible, pray with her and help her to know a loving God instead of the harsh, judging God she had learned about.

Last Saturday, a woman sat in our home and stated firmly that she does not believe that Jesus was God. This same woman, now in her late 60s, was spared from abortion as a baby, escaped death by a bomb when the Germans invaded Russia because "something" inside prompted her to run from where she was hiding, and on many other occasions was kept from death. I know God seeks to woo her to Himself. I was so saddened by her comments that I wanted to cry. Please join me in prayer for her salvation.

At one school, the director told us that he is an atheist but wants to hear the other side of the story. His mother and his *babushka* (grandmother) are believers and he was baptized as a child. He has three sons and he has also had them baptized, though he stated that he does not believe. He seems eager to hear what we have to say and said he hopes several of his teachers will teach the curriculum in their classrooms.

I don't know when I have ever been so challenged. In a nation where even the reality of God was denied they are receiving Christianity with gladness and thanks. Dear friends, we are on the battlefront, whether in Russia, America, or some other country, and our enemy is alive and seeking to kill, steal, and destroy. I challenge you, as never before, to know who you are in Christ, to be clothed in the armor of God, to know the Word of God and to be prayed up! We're not playing a game, we're in battle.

Expecting a great harvest!
Eileen Clay
P.S. It takes about three weeks for mail to arrive, so you may write via e-mail (electronic mail) to eileen@comission.chel.su. It is inexpensive and fast. If you have access to email, I'd enjoy hearing from you. I will need a car when I return home. Please begin now to pray with me that God will provide the right vehicle at the right price.

* * *

Tricia Bullock had answered the still, small voice calling her to salvation in Christ as a sophomore in high school, and later answered that voice into full-time Kingdom work. She graduated from Warner Southern University with a degree in elementary education. At the age of 23, she experienced a strong call to missions.

She spoke about it with her pastor, Ed Nelson, and contacted the Missionary Board of the Church of God. It soon became clear that serving as a special assignment missionary to Chelyabinsk was what God had in mind for Tricia at that point in her life.

Tricia was on the second CoMission team to reach Chelyabinsk. As a Floridian, she was unaccustomed to cold and gloomy weather. As a CoMissioner, she became accustomed to other previously unknown hardships. Leaving Florida with little more than a light jacket and a five-word Russian vocabulary, she headed to Siberia. God provided in mighty ways. Not only did He show Tricia love and protection in all sorts of ways on the journey, but also supplied her with two winter coats.

October 1995

Hello everyone! First of all, I'm happy to report that there IS hot water now that the weather has gotten colder.

I'm not real excited that it's cold; however, the heat and hot water are a plus! Everyone seems to think that this will be a rather cold winter. We had our first snow on September 17! Usually, I'm sweating like crazy in the humid Florida Indian summer, but not now.

I think what really frightens me is that these people who have lived in Siberia all their lives, who are used to the cold and snow, are telling me that this could be a really cold winter. I'm really cold at 60 degrees, I don't even want to think about what they consider cold!

Here in Russia, one of our goals is to meet and greet our neighbors and get them interested in a Bible study of some sort. Well, Connie (my roommate) and I are branching out with some new strategies to meet our neighbors. We were warned that there would be a 24-hour, city-wide water shutdown. Okay, fine, we were thankful for the advance notice.

We filled everything that would hold water. We also filled the tub so we could still flush the toilet. These are important details, trust me! At precisely 4:15 a.m., the doorbell began to ring, shall I say, urgently! I ran through every emotion from pure confusion to paranoia. I couldn't figure out who or what was at the door at this hour, but they didn't sound very friendly.

So I did the only thing that a mature, responsible adult would do. I ran in and woke up my roommate. Not because I was afraid or anything, of course. It's just that she speaks better Russian than I do!

Well, it was our neighbor below on the fourth floor explaining, in no uncertain terms, that there was water, and lots of it, all over their apartment. Oops! I wonder who left the faucet running all this time?

We are full into our semester of classes. We have nine sub-teams of two people teaching the Ethics and Morality curriculum in different areas of the city and three classes of "Level 2." They teach the graduates of the first level how to analyze a Bible passage and write their own plans. This is the class that I co-teach. I teach two times a week for three hours each.

It is so exciting to see how these ladies have grown and to see their desire to learn, not only about teaching methods and ideas, but the Bible and what it means to have a daily time with God. On Tuesday nights, I co—lead a Bible study for young single gals with Nina, the Russian pastor's daughter. I am amazed at what God has done for these ladies and even more amazed as I realize that He is using me for His work. I feel so inadequate, but I wouldn't want to do anything else!

When it was time to head home after her year in Siberia, Tricia prayed that she would still feel that strong dependence on the Lord once she returned to a land where she could speak the language and navigate the culture. She also prepared herself to say good-bye to her 21 year-old brother who was losing a long battle with cancer. He won his prize in the Lord, however, and bequeathed to Tricia yet another compelling example of faith and perseverance. Years later after Tricia married Tim Wiseman, God led the young couple to launch Candlelight Christian Academy in Lake Wales. At the time of writing, this private Christian K-12 school has been educating students for 15 years, including the Wiseman's children, Eli and Adam.

* * *

Connie Callos, Tricia's roommate in 1995, hailed from Vancouver, Washington. She was used to living in a northern climate, but the gray and rainy winters in the U.S. Pacific Northwest offer nothing quite as vigorous as Siberia.

October 1995
Dear family and friends,
How can it be that the time has gone so quickly and November is at hand? One day slips into the next, weeks melt away, and now that far-off time of leaving looms ever larger on the horizon. I say goodbye to Chelyabinsk on December 6 and, following an end-of-year conference in Moscow, arrive back in the Pacific Northwest on December 13.

Though it will be a JOY to go home to family and friends in America, it will not be easy to leave the life and friends God has given me here.

As I walk the streets of this city, or jolt along on a crowded trolley, I watch the changing of autumn into winter and find myself trying to soak in the familiar scenes and faces, the unique look of Russia, a changing Russia. Western influence and Western goods are more and more evident, with all the good and bad they bring. How I wish Russia would take the best of what the West has to offer and not repeat the same mistakes we have made!

I think about Russian children who are learning about the living God who created them and loves them. I think about those who are re-examining their basic assumptions about life in light of what the Bestseller of all time, the Word of God, has to say. I think about those who have heard the good news of Christ for the first time in their life. I think about who I am now, compared to who I was when I came.

Since the beginning of school this fall, I have been co-leading two seminars on the Bible and Christian Ethics and Morality. A class in one region of the city is with a group of 14 teachers from eight different schools. Irena, a Russian chemistry and English teacher who has worked with, and translated for, our team since our arrival two years ago is teaching the latter group with me. It is a joy to be working together, to see her teaching about the things that have become a part of her life in these two years.

Almost half of the women in these classes are believers, while others have not read any of the Bible and are curious to know what it's about. Their enthusiasm, depth of questions, and desire to know is exciting. I find myself looking forward to each class!

Our CoMission team is now 17-strong. As a team, we are leading several Bible seminars for teachers from different regions and schools. We are involved in home Bible study groups, children's neighborhood Bible activities and Bible teaching' outreach to neighboring cities. We make presentations and do teaching at camps, hospitals, orphanages, veterans clubs, women's clubs, and wherever interest is expressed.

As Americans, we like to see results. We like to know what has been accomplished. We find comfort in statistics, but things of God are measured by His standard. If we are faithful to do what He asks of us, through His enabling power, then we can confidently leave the results to Him. He promises His Word will not return void. That is my prayer as my time here draws to a close.

* * *

Orlo and Carol Kretlow were finishing up a 31-year missionary career in Japan when they volunteered for the CoMission. Like their coworkers, they raised the funds necessary to go to Russia, plus a bit more to continue pension and health insurance payments before taking full retirement. As in the case of their coworkers, God provided the resources and the Kretlows found themselves on the second-year CoMission team headed to Chelyabinsk.

November 11, 1995
Dear Friends and Family,
After serving 31 years as missionaries to Japan, we are now serving in a very different culture--Russia. We left Japan in March and came to Chelyabinsk in July.
It has been below freezing for about three weeks. It never thaws. The streets are slippery and we have lots of "black ice" underfoot. Orlo says he has not witnessed really cold weather like this since he left Minnesota at age 18.

On Orlo's birthday in September, we went to the meat market to buy some beef and have a steak dinner, but he changed his mind about that. What an experience! You can buy the whole head of a cow, pig or goat. You choose which part of the beef you want, a piece from the front quarter or hind quarter, and they chop it off for you with a hatchet. If the meat drops on the floor, no problem, they pick it up and wrap it for you. If it is too heavy to carry, they just drag it across the concrete floor.

We decided to buy Tyson chicken legs instead. Carol also bought a Snickers bar for Orlo's birthday present, his favorite. She cut it in half and only let him eat half of it, and then gave him the other half the next day. He thought it was a great birthday gift!

We are teaching a course called "Ethics and Morality, a Foundation For Faith." In late September, we went to the city of Miass about 80 miles away and opened a new program. Some teachers had come to our conferences and asked us to come to their city to offer our course. When we go, we have one three-hour course in the afternoon and then in the evening we have a preaching service. We stay overnight on Friday, and on Saturday we have children's classes. Then we teach another afternoon session and come home. The people appear starved for the Bible.

We are under the "protection" of Vadim Kespikov, the Minister of Education in Chelyabinsk. The school's principal is his wife. The school is near a tractor factory, formerly a tank factory. This factory has not paid its employees since July. They have moved many children in that school into government dormitories. The only food they get is what the school feeds them, and that is not much.

Inflation is very high. It takes everything an average person makes just to put food on the table. We can ride the bus, trolleys and street cars free because we are 62, but we do much walking. You may have to go to several shops to find some item that you need. We looked for a couple weeks to find a broom. The one I saw the other day I did not buy because I thought it was too expensive. Now I cannot find one anywhere. They say, "If you see it buy it, because it will not be there tomorrow."

We experienced how scarcity can lead to impulse buying. We were out one day and discovered small jars of Jiffy peanut butter. We bought two of them and hurried home with our "treat." We put bread in the toaster oven and when it was done we put lots of peanut butter on it. As we were eating the second slice, Carol stopped and said, "What am I doing! I don't even like peanut butter!"

The people that really pull at your heart are the old women pensioners who stand along the street with a little cup. Their widow's pension is so small it is not even enough to buy one loaf of bread a day. Some have some vegetables to sell to make a little money. I always buy my vegetables from them, if I can.

The militia--not the police, but with KGB connection--has been coming to apartments and checking passports and visas. There is a locked door for our hall and a doorbell there. We never let anyone onto the floor that we do not know. When it is a Russian speaker, we have the older Russian couple next door take care of it.

In late October, the bell rang and Orlo went to the door. Russian! So he got the folks next door. The lady called out, "Who is it?" and then just went white and nervous. The militia wanted to see our passports and they absolutely petrified her. She remembers when this meant that they took the men of the house away and you never saw some member of the family again.

To make it short, they took down our information, tipped their hats and left. As they left, the lady was peeking out the door to see if they were carrying us off. She kept muttering about the militia. Poor woman!

They have warned us repeatedly not to talk loudly in public or to be out at night. However, sometimes when we are teaching, we cannot help being out after dark. The streets are dark and it is dark at our apartment entrance. It's strange to look out at night and see no neon lights. Security and safety are real issues.

They heard how we taught English as a Second Language (ESL) in Japan for more than 30 years, so they asked us to start an English class for children in connection with the church. We use some songs and tapes we obtained in the States. This is a great ministry, so we started a class for adults. Our lessons have gone well. It is amazing how this brings in people to the church. An atheist came to our Bible lecture and gave us a rough time, but I believe the Holy Spirit helped us handle it well.

We will be moving in December to another location. The rooms are a little bigger, except the kitchen. Our team of 17 will be a team of three after December 10. Do not worry about us; we are doing well and really excited about the opportunities here. Pray with us that God can use us to build up the church.

Carol and Orlo Kretlow

* * *

A Russian friend who will go unnamed was a high school student when the CoMission began operations. However, he had no chance to attend classes on ethics and morality because both his parents worked in the nuclear science industry. Unlike Chelyabinsk, their city remained closed to outsiders and outside influences.

After graduation, my friend went to Moscow and managed to get a place in a well-known university there. CoMission workers started visiting his campus, not to offer courses on Bible-based morality, but to directly evangelize the students. Those who indicated an interest in knowing more about Jesus were invited to study the CoMission curriculum off campus.

"When I found out that they were offering free soup to anyone who attended their meetings," my friend said, "it was a no-brainer for me. I could use the soup."

Times were tough in the 1990s, even for the sons of nuclear scientists.

"During class I mostly did homework, surreptitiously of course. I was not that interested in the content they were teaching," he admitted.

Eventually my friend did develop an interest in the Bible and its teachings, however. At this writing, he works with a Christian aid and development group based in the UK. According to its mission statement, his organization works to "raise up Christian leaders and build global coalitions to share the gospel and change lives."

I can only imagine how many lives, like my friend's, were transformed in ethics and morality classes taught during the CoMission years. How many more multiplied lives will be changed in years to come, as CoMission alumni spread out across the globe to share what they learned in those classes? Good question. Maybe I will find out when I get to Heaven.

Meanwhile, allow me to share a few more testimonies of Russian lives transformed by the CoMission effort.

Irina the interpreter

One CoMissioner recorded this first-hand account of the struggles that Irina and her family faced, struggles shared by many Russians in the days the CoMission was helping disciple them.

Life is difficult for Irina and her family. More than once she spoke of the difficult situation, and is not completely convinced that Russians' newfound freedom is worth the price. It has come with a heavy price, for sure.

Over the years, Irina's grandmother had saved 6,000 rubles for her retirement days. It was a good savings, enough to buy a car--if that was how she chose to spend it--and have some left over. In the Soviet system it would have been a good nest egg for an elderly person, but not now. Due to inflation, 6,000 rubles is worth slightly more than one U.S. dollar. It will buy very little. The woman's elder years look bleak.

Irina must care for her grandmother. Irina's husband is unemployed. At first I thought it was because 75 percent of the factories in town had closed and he became one of the unemployment statistics. After we became closer to Irina, we learned that her husband is an alcoholic and cannot hold a job.

Irina is a new Christian and a very sensitive woman. She often quoted to us poetry that she had written. It was beautiful and intuitive, although written in her second language. She is indeed gifted.

She said that Eileen Clay is her best friend, because "Eileen told me about Jesus."

Irina the educator

Another friend of the CoMission named Irina faced struggles of a much different nature. Yet, Mrs. Irina Kespikov, wife of Chelyabinsk's Minister of Education, discovered the same answer to her questions and a supernatural power to prevail. This first-hand account was written by a member of the last CoMission team to serve in Chelyabinsk.

Irina is the principal of a school of 1,200 students. It is very crowded, so there are two school sessions per day to relieve the overcrowding. Irina is the only principal for both daily sessions. Her workday begins at 8:00 a.m. and runs to 8:00 p.m.

Irina has a family. In addition to regular classes five days a week, the schools hold extra-curricular activities on Saturdays. The children's parents work in a nearby factory for the most part. During the years of the Cold War, the workers produced tanks. Now they produce tractors. Because Russia is having so many economic problems, the workers received no salary for four months.

Irina says that she tries to maintain an atmosphere that promotes happiness. "When we decided to have the Americans come into our school, some of the parents objected, but they trusted the teachers and administration so they were not very strong in their objections," she explained.

"Then when they visited our classes, they said, 'This is a good program for our children. We agree with you that the Americans should come.'"

Bruce Wilkinson and James Dobson produced a special video to explain the CoMission program to parents. This was extremely helpful in gaining their support.

Still, Irina meets people every day who oppose what is happening at her school. We have documents that authorize us to teach the program, yet most of the old political chiefs are against CoMission and what it is doing. Irina says that, even though Russians celebrate Christmas and Easter, it is difficult for them to have a real understanding of Christianity.

Mrs. Kespikov had become personally acquainted with American Christians during an extended visit to the United States in 1993. While living in

Vancouver, Washington, she attended the Church of God congregation there pastored by Gerald and Rena Marvel.

"When I came to America, it was the first time I took a Bible into my hands. I tried to read it, but it was so difficult for me that I put it away.

"When I became a Christian, I understood that Christians are special people and you communicate with them from your heart. When I was staying with (Gerald and Rena) Marvel, I read and studied and asked them questions in the evenings. The Marvels gave me explanation and Jesus came into my heart.

"I had this inner feeling, and I asked Pastor Marvel to baptize me. I felt it was a special moment in my life.

"I pray and speak to God every day, and every time foreigners come, I feel this all over again. These people are related to me."

Irina certainly made the CoMissioners feel at home upon their arrival in Chelyabinsk. In 1994, she was playing Christian music in her office the day the first team of volunteers came to meet her.

"We found tables set, candles lit, music playing, and a dinner served," Jim Albrecht recalled. "She had invited the directors of every academic department to meet with us and hear us share our purpose in coming.

"Before the meal, she invited me to pray. Just three years before, she would likely have lost her job for such heresy. Such an event could only be described as a direct intervention of God in human affairs."

Irina certainly believes in prayer. That was confirmed when she asked our CoMission team, one of the last to visit her office in Chelyabinsk, to pray.

"Please remember our school in your prayers. It is a special school and I have special teachers. Very often we teach and we communicate what is in our hearts with words. So I would like to thank you, because you are the ones who started this teaching here."

At this point, Irina presented each one of us with a small painted cup. "We have a tradition here of giving presents," she said. "I hope when you look at this cup you will pray for us that our work will be better.

"But my first words of thanks are to God. God unites all of us. I have become a happy person."

Ludimida

"The first Christian to come to our school was Eileen Clay," recalls this first-grade teacher in Chelyabinsk.

"At first, not all the teachers in the school were glad that this type of program was beginning, but we think that that was normal. Even though the teachers were not entirely enthusiastic, they supported the program because they respect (school principal) Irina. Eileen and Irina began to work with the teachers and taught Bible.

"We saw the result of their work in the lives of the children. They became more kind and loving, so we wanted to continue. Irina asked the American teachers to teach the teachers instead of the children so that we could continue the program when the Americans left.

"Four teachers learned the curriculum. Every week Eileen helped them make lesson plans. She attended the lessons they taught and discussed how the lesson was done. Teaching the Bible must come from the heart, not from the mind, so four teachers were chosen who would teach from the heart.

"Now, when all the Americans leave, we can still teach the Bible. The seeds that are planted will grow and bear fruit."

Ludmilla

One day in May 1996, a team of CoMissioners visited Ludmilla's third-grade classroom and heard a moving personal lesson about faith and hope. One of the team took notes on the class and passed them along to us. I share them here to illustrate the highly personal teaching methods, rarely encountered in classrooms in the West, which Russian teachers used to creatively communicate Biblical truths to their charges.

My grandmother turned 90 years old in May of this year. When she was 27 years old, her husband died. She had two children when he died, and during the early years after his death she was very hungry because there was not enough money to buy food. But in the spring of the year, there was hope. Food became more plentiful because leaves could be found and made into soup. I asked my granny how she made it through these difficult years, and she told me it was because of faith and hope.

As a child, and for many years after reaching adulthood, I thought that my granny was referring to women whose names were Faith and Hope. These are very popular names for women in Russia. When I became older, I began to understand that the faith and hope that my grandmother told me about were not women who had helped her, but something else. I tried to understand this, but I could not.

One day some Christians came to visit us. They began to speak about faith and hope just like my granny. These Christians lived so far away, but they spoke of the same things as my granny, about faith and hope in God. I am excited about what I have learned.

Our topic today is hope and faith. It is very important to begin to understand these words, so I have some questions for the class.

When you face difficulties, where can you find some answers for your difficult questions? You can find the answers in the Bible, the Word of life, the most important book.

What is prayer? It is conversation with God.

Let's look at what we read in the Bible about hope and faith. Read Hebrews, Chapter 11, silently. Try to remember what is hope and faith. It says it is impossible to please God without faith. Why?

We have many examples from the Bible of people who have had faith. Do you know examples?

Noah believed in God. Everyone laughed at Noah, but he believed in God. There is also Abraham, Moses and Jonah.

Now let us look at hope. What do you understand about hope? Let's read Romans 12:12, "Be joyful in hope, patient in affliction, faithful in prayer." Now we read Romans 15:13, "May the God of hope fill you with all joy and peace as you trust in him, so that you may overflow with hope by the power of the Holy Spirit." I would like for you to remember this, and so we will make a dove. When you are finished, let your dove fly to my island. I will give you a green leaf of hope.

Marina

The next stop on the CoMissioners' itinerary that day was Marina's second-grade classroom. They also took notes on her lesson plan and passed them along to us. As in the case of Ludmilla, Marina used very personal stories to convey the essence of the lesson to her young pupils.

"What is a key?" Marina asks. "It is something that we use to unlock a lock, but there is also another meaning to 'key' that we would like to talk about.

"I have brought many keys with me today." Marina shows the class a large key ring with all shapes and sizes of keys. "We use keys to open doors and all kinds of things. Look at the box I have here. What do you think is in the box?"

The children offer several answers. It could be more keys, or books, or maybe the Word of Life. Let's have a look.

"Yes, you are right! The Word of Life is in the box. In Matthew 16:19, Jesus says, 'I will give you the keys of the kingdom.' What are these keys? What is the kingdom? Where is this kingdom?"

The children again offer several answers.

"It is the kingdom of kindness."

"It is the kingdom of justice and good."

"It is the kingdom of faith."

"It is the kingdom of truth."

Marina resumes. "Let me draw you a picture. Where can you find the keys to get to heaven?"

"If you follow God's commandments."

"Maybe if you pray."

"We must do what God wants us to do."

"We must have faith, hope and love."

Marina resumes. "The key is faith. We must have special keys to open this kingdom. The Bible will help us find the keys." The children open their Bibles and find a piece of a puzzle in each Bible.

"What did you find?" their teacher asks. The students work together to make the puzzle and when they finish, it forms the shape of a key. The words of the Lord's Prayer are written on the puzzle.

"Who knows by heart this prayer?" Marina asks. "Don't just say this prayer, or read it without thinking about the words. If you really say the words with faith, you will know the truth, and it will open the keys of the kingdom.

"I would like you to open something for me. Let's try to open my heart. I think that for my heart, these keys on my key ring will not work. There is a special key for the heart."

Marina brings out a pretty box and uses a key to open it. In the box was a red heart attached to a necklace that she put on. Marina told the children about Jesus being the key to open our hearts. She opened the necklace's heart and there was a picture of Jesus. She talked about Jesus coming into our hearts and then had each child cut out a key-shaped book mark to help them remember the lesson.

* * *

I, for one, am grateful to those CoMissioners for taking detailed notes that day in the classrooms of Ludmilla and Marina. It was one of the last opportunities to chronicle first-hand how Russian teachers were adapting the ethics and morality curriculum. The following year, CoMission volunteers ceased going to Russia.

More would have gone, I am sure, had the program continued. But that was impossible, given the political and religious realities in the Russian Federation at the time. Already in the autumn of 1993, ominous clouds gathered over the CoMission when the Russian parliament proposed legislation restricting "foreign" religious activity. Bishops of the Russian Orthodox Church threatened to withdraw their support of President Boris Yeltsin unless he agreed to support the law. Yeltsin dissolved Parliament before it could take action, not because of this issue, it should be mentioned. Nevertheless, a precedent had been established.

Russian politicians cannot easily defy the will of the Orthodox Church. In terms of world Christianity, it is second only to the Roman Catholic Church in number of adherents. Polls indicate that half to three-quarters of the Russian population identify themselves as Orthodox adherents. That is a lot of votes.

Under Patriarch Alexy II, who became Primate (Archbishop) of Moscow in 1990, Orthodox Christianity made a strong comeback into Russian society after 70 years of exclusion. He and his cohorts transformed the Russian Orthodox Church into something resembling a state religion, re-opening or constructing 15,000 churches by the end of his tenure. Zealous to protect their religious community from outside competition, Orthodox clergy teamed with nationalist politicians to push through legislation that eventually restricted the migration of religious workers from other countries and limited their length of stay in Russia.

However, politics was not the only reason--not even the primary reason, in fact--that CoMission ceased operating. Wilkinson, Eshleman and other leaders in the organization wisely calculated that the door into Russia's public schools would not remain open indefinitely. Like other effective mission strategists, they built a beginning, middle and end into the design of CoMission, passing the torch to local leaders once they had completed their agenda.

They conceived a five-year time frame for the initiative, the typical start-up phase for international mission projects. If you have achieved something by then, strategists reckon, its own momentum will carry it forward. If your project fails, extending it into an indefinite future is not likely to produce anything of eternal value.

CoMission was certainly not a failure, and evidence suggests that it created many things of eternal value in Russia, in the United States, and beyond. For five years, 87 church denominations and mission agencies worked together to provide intensive Bible teaching to Russian educational leaders, youth and families. Few modern Christian movements have achieved that kind of purposeful unity. "We have worked together for five years, and no one has gotten mad or walked off," Bruce Wilkinson stated succinctly. "There has been a wonderful sense of cooperation and unity."

Cooperation and unity translated into notable achievements. Between 1992 and 1998, more than

1,500 CoMission volunteers spent a year each in Russia teaching Christian Ethics and Morality to students and educators. Meanwhile, the organization sponsored 136 teacher convocations in 116 cities across the former Soviet Union. These meetings drew a total of 41,618 participants, all of whom viewed the *JESUS* film and received additional orientation for teaching the Christian Ethics and Morality curriculum. An estimated 10 to 11 million students participated in classes based on the Ten Commandments and the teachings of Jesus. Most of those students heard the gospel presented for the first time in their lives.

For its part, the Church of God succeeded in deploying the 50 CoMission volunteers that Norm Patton had pledged to send to Chelyabinsk and the nearby mining city of Miass. They communicated the Bible message to hundreds of school children and scores of teachers in the local schools. CoMissioners also developed relationships with Russians in all levels of society--universities, medical and nursing schools, government agencies and business circles.

With characteristic attention to detail, Jim Albrecht listed some of the achievements that CoMission attained.

> The lasting success of the CoMission project is not due to any one individual or group. The leaders of the CoMission were all full-time directors of some of the largest Christian ministries in the world. They gave freely of their time and energy to see the project succeed.
>
> As a representative of the Missionary Board of the Church of God, it was my privilege to sit at CoMission Executive Committee meetings to plan, pray and strategize. There was a deep spiritual tone to all of these meetings. There was a sense of awe that God was working far beyond what we could ask

or think. This was a providential moment in time, when God lit a fire that is still burning.

The Church of God was mobilized to action as never before in our history. Each of the 50 Special Assignment Missionaries raised his or her own budget from individuals and churches and enlisted 50 or more prayer partners.

To keep their supporters informed by email, every team took laptop computers with them and maintained constant contact. This was the first time this happened on such a scale. They took VCR players, monitors and other equipment to share the *JESUS* film, as well as Bibles, biblical study literature and teaching materials.

Every team member lived a Russian lifestyle, renting apartments among the local people and shopping at neighborhood markets. They did not elevate themselves to "rich Westerner" status, which contributed greatly to their acceptance and success. Everyone participated in pre-field orientation, and mid-term debriefing and R&R. A psychiatrist met with the teams on more than one occasion and counseling was available when needed.

The Church of God was one of the few CoMission organizations to plant a church, which achieved official government registration in December 1995. At that time, Kelley Philips and I met with Chelyabinsk Mayor, Slava Tarasov, and Director of Education, Vadim Kespikov, to sign a new 10-year protocol agreement.

"You Americans have brought a spirit of hope to our people," Mayor Tarasova commented at the protocol signing. "Thank you for coming."

The total financial investment in the CoMission amounted to three-quarters of a million dollars. It was a God-gift that when the effort ended, every bill was paid and the CoMission was $10,000 in the black. The Missionary Board had greatly reduced its overall indebtedness, as well, which amounted to a kind of dividend for its sponsorship of the venture.

All of this says to me that when God is in our plans, we need to make them big. God is still moving among his people to see lasting results. Who knows where this will all lead?

Norm Patton strongly agreed with Jim on this point. "God has helped me to understand that when He gives you a vision of what He wants done, trust Him to bring it to pass," he wrote as the Church of God Missionary Board was winding down the CoMission work.

"He has done it in an amazing way, and so many persons have been obedient to Him to bring about this ministry. Thank you, Lord, for stretching my faith and vision in Phoenix."

* * *

What continues to mystify me a quarter century after these events is why God chose a 28-year-old youth pastor and six Florida teens to open a door to Siberia. On the other hand, I have come to believe that when we walk with God in daily discipline, He opens up doors and opportunities that challenge the imagination. We give Him full credit for what happened in Chelyabinsk 25 years ago and what is happening there today. I can only echo Paul's words in Ephesians 3:21, "to him be glory in the church and in Jesus Christ throughout all generations, forever and ever. Amen."

Even though our trips to Chelyabinsk had opened the door for Church of God volunteers to join the CoMission movement, I personally never joined a CoMission team. In fact, Vickie and I led the last mission trip from Florida to Chelyabinsk five months *before* the first Missionary Board-sponsored CoMission team left for Russia.

The New Way Singers musical group was part of this August 1993 mission team. A fair number of pastors joined us as well, including Ken Long, the lead pastor at Vero Beach Church of God where I was now working as a minister to students. Ken remembers that the trip provided some genuine eye-opening experiences for him.

"My grandfather was a member of the John Birch Society, so I grew up with the anti-Communist rhetoric," he told me. "The Lord seemed to take me deliberately to places to set me free from these previously held prejudices.

"I remember the occasion when I went to the home of our interpreter, Valentina, for dinner, and I shared this detail with her. She looked at me hesitantly and said, 'My husband is a Communist. How do you feel about us now?'

"At that moment, the Lord did a work in my heart that replaced those long-held feelings with a genuine love for the people there.

"It was still so early in the process of [Russia's] opening up to the gospel. It felt like the days of the apostle Paul, especially on the train going through the towns and villages. The crowds of people at the stations who apparently had not seen a Westerner for 70 years will always be remembered.

"Everywhere we went, we sang. Music is truly a universal language. I loved the concert the kids did."

That concert was one of several that Florida's New Way Singers performed along the way. High points of the 14-day journey were the evening worship services with New Way Singers leading many of the songs. Our interaction with students and city leaders continued to build the relationships we had established. We had wonderful discussions with Vadim and Irina Kespikov, Alexander Popov, Albert Akmalov and many faculty members at Lyceum #31. Although it did not feel like it, it turned out to be my last trip to Siberia for many years to come.

* * *

In those days, God was opening doors to Russia at break-neck speed. It soon became clear to all involved that it would be good for a career missionary to move to Chelyabinsk to assist the CoMission teams and shepherd the newly planted church in the city. As early as April of 1992, people were encouraging my family to consider this assignment. Ed Nelson, Norm Patton, Jim Albrecht, the president of my alma mater, Warner University, and many other influential persons in our lives were suggesting that Vickie and I pray about accepting a missionary posting to Russia. After all, I was responsible for beginning the venture. It only made sense that the Shaner family should follow it through.

Vickie and I had been married for 10 years by this time and were parents of an 8-year-old daughter, Gina, and 4-year-old Zach. We had settled the issue a long time ago that we would do whatever God asked of us. We were open to God's direction. If Russia was what God wanted for us, we would be obedient to that call.

We spent a number of months in the land of indecision. Then in January of 1993, it all suddenly changed.

In those days, the youth ministry of the Church of God in Florida was very connected, organizing an annual state-wide convention on Thanksgiving weekend and an ongoing training program known as the Student Leadership Institute. Youth workers in the state were well acquainted with one another, thanks to the ministry of Don Pickett, Director of the Florida Youth Fellowship.

Kelley Philips was one of those Florida youth workers, serving a congregation in Jacksonville. Unbeknownst to me, Kelley had gone to the USSR with

Josh McDowell in the 1980's to pass out Bibles on the streets of Moscow and St. Petersburg. Afterward, he tried to convince his wife Rhonda to move to the USSR because the Soviets were so hungry for God's Word. Rhonda listened but remained unconvinced.

"Kelley," she finally said in exasperation, "I'll do three all-night lock-ins with the youth group this year, if you will just put that thought out of your mind!"

Then Kelley and Rhonda volunteered to help chaperon the Chelyabinsk delegation that visited the United States in November of 1992. Vickie and I were among the greeters who met the Russians upon their arrival in Washington, D.C., and then I flew home to stay with the children. Vickie, Cheri Nelson and the Philipses accompanied the visitors on the bus trip down the east coast and through the state of Florida. During those two weeks aboard the bus, they watched God melt Russian and American hearts together in an extraordinary way. Rhonda Philips was so moved by the experience that when we took the Russians to the airport after Thanksgiving to fly home, she was ready to get on the plane and fly home with them!

By the following January, while Ed Nelson and Ron Beard were in Chelyabinsk discipling the new believers who would eventually coalesce into a flourishing church, pressure on Vickie and me to make a decision about becoming career missionaries to Siberia had intensified to the tipping point. "God," I said, "If you want me in Russia, I'll go. But I have to know."

One Friday morning I went to the beach to pray and wait on the Lord. I got there at 6:00 a.m. and told God I would not leave the beach until I heard from Him exactly what He wanted me to do. I also promised Him that whatever that thing was, I would do it.

I walked up and down the beach for three hours. Right around 9:00 a.m., I heard that still, small voice say, "Some plant, some water and some harvest. You have done what I asked you to do, now get out of the way."

And then I believe I heard God say, "... Or you will mess it up!"

I left the beach and headed to my office, satisfied that the Lord had told me that I was not the person for a missionary assignment in Chelyabinsk. I walked in, sat down at my desk and within 30 minutes the phone rang. It was Kelley Philips, wondering if we could get together. He did not tell me why. I told him that I was free the following Monday and could meet him in Titusville at the Dixie Crossroads restaurant for lunch.

On Monday, I met Kelley as planned. Once we were seated in a booth, I asked him what was up. He slid a copy of "Church of God Missions" magazine across the table, one that featured the latest news on Russia, and said, "I believe God is calling me and my family to be career missionaries to Russia. Do you think we could do it?"

I stared at him, open-mouthed. The answer could not have been more obvious. Not only were Vickie and I not to go to Chelyabinsk, it was clear that God had prepared Kelley and Rhonda to take up the baton and carry on the work.

The following October, the Philips family left for their first five-year missionary term in Chelyabinsk with their two children, Lee, 11, and Lindsay, 8. To their lasting credit, they meshed favorably with the Russian people, learning the language so well and adapting to the culture so naturally that they nearly became Russian themselves.

Kelley took with him a vision of a strong indigenous church, self-supporting and self-propagating. He succeeded in reaching those goals in a remarkable way. By 2002 the Philips had worked themselves out of a job, as every good missionary endeavors to do. They left Chelyabinsk with a church led by two Russian pastors, pursuing the believers' vision of planting new congregations in surrounding towns and villages.

I don't know if the Shaners could have been as successful as the Philipses in shepherding the Chelyabinsk church through its infancy and into maturity, but that is a moot point now. I do know that I am eternally grateful that I heard and heeded God's voice on that Florida beach, when He said that I had finished my part in this story and it was time for me to get out of the way.

* * *

I cannot write first-hand about the church that was planted and grew up in Chelyabinsk. That story belongs to Kelley and Rhonda Philips and the believers in Siberia who have met Jesus and faithfully follow Him. Perhaps one day they will write their own book. I hope so.

I did learn one part of that story, however, that I want to share here. It illustrates how God works and the kinds of things that come of his plans. The story belongs to a young woman named Ekaterina.

I was born in Kopeysk, a small city near Chelyabinsk, to hard-working, middle-class parents. My father was a policeman, my mother a violin teacher and later director of a music school. We had a bunch of friends and dear grandparents, but no God in our lives.

One of our relatives, however, invited my mother to create a choir at the Church of God in Chelyabinsk, so she added another job to her already busy schedule. For a while, the church was just a place of fun, with a sense of community and fellowship. It was like a family that you love and grow up with together. Then my mother became a believer, and my sister Yana and I followed in her footsteps.

It was apparent from the beginning that we would have to stand for our faith in the midst of an unbelieving generation. My father, a Muslim, decided to divorce my mother. My grandmother tried to stop Mother from being baptized with the words, "If you get baptized, you are not welcome in my home."

But none of these trials quenched my mother's desire to follow Jesus.

At my conversion, the Lord revealed Himself to me--as He often does to persons of Muslim heritage--through a dream. I saw an ancient lamp made of stars and the Light inside the lamp. That warm, almost liquid light represented Jesus. I saw the earth pass by and the Light illuminating the surrounding darkness. After this, I began to share about Jesus with friends and classmates at school. They were intrigued and some came to the church.

My sister had her own journey of faith. Even at her young age, she sensed that something was not right in the world. Something was missing. When she came to the church and found Jesus, He filled the void that she felt! She found peace and love.

From the get-go our family was in the church music ministry and remains so to this day. We are Levites in houses of the Lord, all three of us attending different congregations as God willed. Yet our hearts are full of praise and worship to Jesus for who He is.

Unbeknownst to us, Father God was preparing a journey for me to America, though I had never chased that dream. I found myself drawn to the Bible in my free time and longed to study it more deeply. The only other desire I had was to learn to draw and become an interior designer. I joined some drawing classes at the university in Chelyabinsk while attending high school.

By this time, Mother had remarried a man who is a believer and my family decided that I should move to St. Petersburg to finish high school. Literally in the space of a few days, I was thrust into a new city and a new school, without parents or church. I did not complain about the change. My dependence on God grew.

It was a co-ed lyceum of girls and boys. The students lived, ate and studied on campus, so I had a roommate. Since I joined the lyceum community in the last few months before graduation, I was like a new shoot among well-grown trees. I began to write poetry, pray and read the Word. That dependence on Jesus caused others to be drawn to me. They came to ask for prayer, to confess their sins and seek holiness. I did not strive to be the leader in any of these arenas. I was simply holding on to Jesus.

After graduation, I enrolled in university in St. Petersburg to study public relations. I did not have a clear picture of what I wanted to do in life, but this sounded like a good job for the future. For the next two years, my life was the university and the new Korean Presbyterian church I attended.

In early 2004, my stepfather sent my mother to St. Petersburg with instructions to pay the tuition for the rest of that academic year. My mother was in line to pay, when I left her side to retrieve some documents from another office. I had an unusual encounter with a classmate on the way.

This person came to me and gently took my hands. "*Katusha*," she said, using an affectionate nickname, "are you leaving the university?"

I stood there dumbfounded. I could feel the literal presence of Jesus coming through this person. When I returned to my mother, I asked, "Mother, did anything happen while I was gone?"

She replied, "The Holy Spirit spoke to me and

said, 'Why are you paying if she is going to study abroad.' He repeated it three times. I replied that I was simply doing what my husband had asked of me."

We paid the tuition for rest of the year, but left the university extremely excited about something which we could not yet fully grasp. We returned home, convinced that God would speak to us. How? It did not matter. Something miraculous was happening. My mother began to pray and she heard the Lord saying to her: "She will study in America. Bible, psychology and pedagogy."

He continued, "Women, children, a family and families." Three times she heard the words "anointing of the Holy Spirit," and then a call to love everybody.

Well, it was clear that I was to study in America. Six months later, I landed in the United States and began my studies at Anderson University in Indiana.

In 2005, my daughter Gina was in her sophomore year at Anderson University when I was invited to speak one morning in the college chapel. The theme of my message was 1 Corinthians 1:26-29, how God uses the foolish things of the world to confound the wise.

As part of my remarks, I told the story of God using six high school students and a youth pastor to birth a church in a city once dedicated to military research and weapons development in the former Soviet Union.

At the close of the chapel service, a student came down the aisle with tears in her eyes. It was Ekaterina. She told me how, as a middle-school student in Chelyabinsk, she had given her life to Christ while attending the church that started with our visit in 1991. She had never heard, until today, the story of how the church was planted that eventually introduced her to the Lord. She could not stop expressing, through tears of joy, her gratitude for what we had been a part of back then. "Thank you, thank you, thank you," she said, multiple times.

It was a moment I will never forget.

Ekaterina graduated from AU in 2008. Later she attended Anderson School of Theology, graduating with a Master's of Intercultural Service in 2011. On May 28 of that year, she married Samuel Lewis Green. At this writing, the couple has a 4-year-old son and a 2-year-old daughter.

The Greens are active in New Life Christian Church in Anderson, a congregation that regularly sends short-term mission teams to Russia. They primarily work among the Kalmyk people, an ethnic group just recently reached by the gospel.

"It is a privilege to serve alongside missionaries and servants of the Lord in both the United States and Russia," Ekaterina said. "I find myself reflecting on the truth that, in two different cultural settings, one thing is needed to reach the world with the gospel: to follow Jesus in obedience and put Him first above all things."

* * *

I currently live on a street in Anderson, Indiana, called Ripple Drive. I consider that a happy coincidence as I write this book. A "ripple," according to the dictionary, is "a small wave or series of waves on the surface of water, especially as caused by an object dropping into it or a slight breeze." I have come to realize that this book is about the ripple effect of a group of teens providentially dropped into a foreign and faraway city as the wind of the Holy Spirit was moving over the land.

Twenty years after my first excursion into Siberia, I got to visit Chelyabinsk again and see how far the ripples had radiated outward. In July 2011, I helped organize a group of 40 American teens and youth workers to hold an English Camp with 60 of our

Russian counterparts. We camped together in tents on a lake near Chelyabinsk.

While there, I visited Lyceum #31 to reconnect with the school's headmaster, Alexander Popov. My friend Logan Ritchhart filmed a conversation between Alexander and myself, conducted through an interpreter.

Alexander let me know that the previous month he was in Moscow at the Kremlin, sitting at a table with Vladimir Putin. The Russian president awarded Lyceum #31 the rank of third-best school in all of Russia, after lyceums in St. Petersburg and Moscow.

Alexander told me that many of his graduates had since immigrated to the United States to take jobs at NASA, the Pentagon, and a variety of other government agencies and private businesses. At this writing, his daughter Vica is living in New York and works in the financial industry.

"There are physicists in Florida from my school, mathematicians in Tennessee, and computer programmers in Pennsylvania and New York," Alexander said. "They are quite noticeable and famous. I am proud of them."

"Don't worry," he added, with a sly grin. "We taught them to be the best mathematicians in the world, but not to get wrapped up in the political process."

I asked Alexander if our visit in 1991 had somehow influenced these students and the direction they had taken.

"You did a great deal, because you showed our students that the world is open for communication," he replied. "We had never been abroad, most of us, and we thought that other people were absolutely different from us.

"But when we met you, we saw that we were the same--same smiles, same arms and legs. Our meetings and discussions actually quieted our anxiety about the safety of our world. What was left was joy from the communication."

Alexander presented me with copies of three mathematics books he had written, all in Russian. Although, I confess, I am not particularly wired to understand mathematics, I treasure them.

I learned that Alexander Popov still treasures a book I gave him in 1991.

"I had never had a personal copy of the Bible," he said. "But when you came, I got my personal Bible. I still have it. I still read it, every day.

"At that time it was impossible to buy Bibles, or even to find a Bible. But you brought so many Bibles and showed us how to study it.

"Before your arrival, our favorite book at Lyceum #31 was *Elements* by the ancient Greek mathematician Euclid. That was Number One book for us. But after you came, the second Number One book--or maybe the first--was the Bible.

"Bible is one of the greatest books of the world. Every person should know this book, should read this book."

It was a wonderful experience for me to catch up again with this highly accomplished educator and civic leader, who still held the Bible in high regard and repeated his assertion that I was the one who taught him to think with his heart.

It was on that visit in 2011 that I first heard the stories of Gertruda Deimler and Nelly Schule, the two German women who grew up in the Chelyabinsk area following their fathers' internment in World War II. Their testimonies of living as "underground believers" through the Stalin era (related in Part Two of this book) greatly enriched our fellowship with Russian Christians during the visit.

Gertruda, now a 73-year-old great-grandmother, said, "I was overfilled with joy when I heard there was a Church of God established in Chelyabinsk. I could not find the right words, or fully understand the goodness of God and His ways.

"When I learned that Walentin Schule was planning to visit Chelyabinsk, I pleaded with him to take me with him. I'm just thrilled to see that the church in Chelyabinsk can do so many wonderful things, and you don't have any restrictions.

"Now having been here, I will be praying for you."

Nelly Schule, now 78 and a grandmother, echoed Gertruda's enthusiasm.

"At the time we lived here, we were not allowed to have church. Now I have been to Ukraine five times for a [Bible] conference, to Estonia three times, and I am very happy to have come back to Chelyabinsk.

"There are people in Germany who come to Chelyabinsk for conferences and there are people in Chelyabinsk who have visited us in Germany.

"I'm just delighted to stay connected to this church. It's a lot of work, so I pray the Lord will give me extra strength, extra health, and I can be productive in His Kingdom."

Andrey Kolegov, a leading elder of the Russian Church of God, said, "These brave men and women did not pray [back in the 1950s] for a Russian church to appear in Chelyabinsk. That prospect was absolutely unimaginable to them. Their goal was simply to stay alive and remain faithful.

"They were despised by Russians as Fascists who had no right to speak into their lives. But God honored their faith. We see a spiritual connection to these roots. We are one family."

The Chelyabinsk church hopes to plant a new congregation in Kopeysk where several families of German background still reside. Russian Christians feel a duty to do all they can to establish a church in the place where, despite horrible hardship, faith was kept alive by believers who risked their lives to follow Jesus.

* * *

American Christians in this story are also following Jesus 25 years later, albeit without risk to our lives. Like ripples on water, our journeys have taken directions very different from what we could have imagined. Stephanie Muhlenforth Barber said our initial trip to Chelyabinsk in 1991, "opened the doors to a whole new world for me."

"Coming from a small town has its limitations," she explained. "However, having the opportunity to travel to Chelyabinsk broadened my world view, not only personally, but also in the way I pursue my career, my marriage and my parenting style. I'm more likely to think outside the box and be more accepting to those who are different from me.

"The ability to serve in that capacity has made me a better leader, a more positive person, and blessed me with the ability to overcome hardships and difficulties. My walk with Jesus became more of a relationship on that trip and has continued since."

Stephanie has pursued a career in secondary education, for 20 years in the classroom as a teacher to special needs students, and most recently as Assistant Principal of River Ridge High School in Woodstock, Georgia. She is the wife of Michael Barber, a New Way Singers alumnus who visited Chelyabinsk in 1993 and again in 2001.

The Barbers are raising their two school-age children in the Atlanta area, where they are active in Legacy Church (formerly Town Center Community Church). Stephanie has served the congregation's youth and children's ministries, and also as an executive on the elder board.

"I am currently pursuing a specialist degree in leadership from Berry College," she said. "Michael and I are a part of a leadership team that initiated the creation of Legacy Church in the Canton/Marietta area."

Shawn Brown's experience in Chelyabinsk inspired him to take Russian language classes during his studies at the University of Florida, but that was not the only impact on him.

"Like all trips out of country, it made me more appreciative of what we have here," he said. "The lack of space and food is something that will stick with me forever.

"It certainly expanded my views on Christianity outside of our country and how far behind we are as a nation in education, particularly given the resources we have.

"Another thing that will always stick with me is the generosity and kindness afforded by our guests, and this despite not having Christianity in their lives."

Shawn and his wife, Christina Vogel Brown, live in Sarasota, Florida and are the parents of one son and a daughter. Shawn works as a sales and marketing executive, and the couple operates a gymnasium specializing in the Olympic sports of Judo/Jiu-Jitsu and gymnastics.

Greg Campbell, the 14-year-old student who was entrusted to my care by his widowed mother, updated me about how his life continues to follow the ripples that God stirred up in Russia.

"Before the trip, God hadn't yet told me what He wanted me to do, so I decided I would work toward going to the Air Force Academy until I heard otherwise. I'd be a pilot for 20 years--F16's of course--and then get a job flying a corporate jet. At age 40, I'd have military retirement and health care benefits for me, my wife and any children that came along. It seemed like a good plan.

"The summer of 1991, after the trip, I felt a call to missions. The desire to have a military career ended."

That same summer, Greg served as a junior counselor at a children's camp in Leesburg, Florida, where he met fellow camp counselor Becki Bartels. It proved to be another life-changing experience.

The pair dated throughout their respective college careers, Becki's at Anderson University and later at Warner University in Lake Wales, and Greg at Stetson University in Deland, Florida, where he completed two years of studies in international business and Russian. The couple married in 1997, following Becki's return from a teaching stint in Haiti. In 2002, Greg earned a B.S. degree in Christian Leadership from Johnson University in preparation for what has become the Campbell family's calling: urban missions.

Greg and Becki lived in the inner city of Orlando for the first eight years of their marriage, sharing their lives and resources with the community. At one point, they found themselves providing a roof over the heads of neighborhood kids who needed a place to live, while raising their own one-year-old daughter.

"A dictum that is often attributed to St. Francis of Assisi became very real," Greg said. 'Preach the gospel, and if necessary, use words.' I have learned that there is value in simply living out one's faith. As Mark used to tell us, 'Your Walk talks, and your Talk walks, but your Walk talks louder than your Talk walks.'

"When I started my current employment in 2000, it was with the expectation that our family would eventually go overseas, but that didn't happen. I think that our part in the story is to serve in the church here, strengthening families and serving as a catalyst for those going to other parts of the world."

Greg and Becki have helped plant two Orlando churches, Living Waters Community Church of God and Restoration Community Church. Today, the Campbells have three daughters and a son and worship at Good Shepherd Catholic Church, a multi-ethnic, multi-lingual congregation that serves families from around the world.

Melanie Newcomer Miller holds a nursing degree from Goshen College in Indiana. Following missionary service in Honduras, she and husband Mark settled in Broadway, Virginia, where Melanie works as a Spanish-English interpreter. The Millers have three adolescent children and are active in the *Iglesia Discipular Anabaptista* (Anabaptist Discipleship Church) and Grace Mennonite Fellowship.

"As humans, we are all so similar when it comes down to the basics of hopes and dreams, goals and desires," Melanie said, reflecting on the impact of her experience in Chelyabinsk. "What so many see as barriers and differences that divide, can be laid aside when we touch the heart of another person.

"I have seen this over and over again in my life, whether as a child living with my missionary family in Guatemala, or as an adult serving as a missionary myself in Honduras, or today as I work in clinics for the underprivileged and provide interpretation services to people living in a country that is not their own.

"So I endeavor to organize my life around relationships, investing in time--face time, not Facebook--and in the lives of those God brings into my day. My life is filled to overflowing with the beauty of friendship, and for this I am a better person."

Melanie has maintained a life-long friendship with her fellow travelers, Sara and Karis. All three are married with families and live in different states, yet they still keep in touch and try to visit as often as they can.

Sara Fasel Kane earned a bachelor's degree from Anderson University; a master's from Florida State University, and at this writing is working on a Doctorate of Education at Florida Southern College. She serves as Dean of Records and Registrar at Warner University and lives in Lake Wales with husband Stephen and their two children. The Kane family is active in Holy Spirit Catholic Church.

"At a young age, my parents instilled in me a love of travel and cross-cultural experiences," she said. "Yet on this adventure at age 15, God revealed in me a deep love for the hearts of His children and a peace that traverses all worldly boundaries.

"We had the opportunity to create deep, meaningful friendships. I regret that we didn't have social media in the 1990s which could have kept us better connected with our Russian counterparts. I treasure the letters we exchanged and long for the day I might be reunited with each of my friends."

"I did not meet Sara and Melanie until a few days before we left for Russia, but came home with a life-long bond to them," Karis Blunden Madison said. "They knew and understood what I had been through, so I sought their company often. Sara asked me to be her maid of honor when she married in 2006."

Karis, a homemaker who homeschools her son Isaac, earned her B.A. degree from Asbury University and an M.S. in Family Studies from the University of North Carolina at Greensboro. She and husband Dan Madison live in McCordsville, Indiana, where Karis is active in several women's ministries.

When asked about life lessons she learned in Chelyabinsk that she would like to pass on to teens today, Karis said, "Basically, the message of 1 Timothy 4:12, don't let being young stop you from thinking you can make a difference. Sometimes being less set in your ways makes you a better instrument for God's purposes.

"I came home viewing myself as a leader and have taken on various leadership roles in school, college and church ministry ever since. The trip chipped away at my egocentrism and made me aware that there is always another side to the story."

Karis says the Russian experience also pushed her to be prepared to make a defense to anyone when called to account for the hope within.

"When I was a freshman in college, my family hosted a friend from Chelyabinsk named Sasha who was traveling through the States. He was not one that joined the new believers there, and remained very skeptical of religion.

"One day, he pointedly confronted me, saying, 'If you had grown up in a Muslim family, you would be a good Muslim girl.' In other words, my faith was merely part of my culture, nothing more.

"This was both hurtful and helpful to me. It's true that I was not one to question the order of things, I had a compliant nature. So my Russia experience provided someone outside my close-knit Christian world to push me to confront, not only what I believe, but also why I believe it."

* * *

I may have authored this book but a lot of other people helped write the story. Because of their obedience to God, many remarkable things came to pass for which I will always be grateful.

First of all, I want to emphasize that God did it. No one gathered in a boardroom to plan it out, or formed a committee to make it happen. God just did it. He opened the door and used a whole lot of people through a miraculous chain of events to establish His church in this city in the Ural Mountains.

He did it through the prayers and dreams of a tiny group of German believers who landed there during World War II. Years later He brought into the story a Shreveport, Louisiana youth minister who traveled all the way to the Soviet Union seeking the finest treatment he could find for his injured daughter. Then this man extended an invitation to another youth minister praying in the woods in central Florida, asking God to use him to make a difference.

Yet, that invitation would not have produced our student exchange trip to Russia had not Don Pickett set protocol aside and risked his reputation to give a young upstart like me a shot at doing something crazy for God. It fell to my pastor Ed Nelson to give me the thumbs up to go ahead with this impossible dream. If he had not agreed, the first word of the story you have just read would never have been written.

I will be forever grateful to Dr. Jim Albrecht for recognizing that a wide door had opened for effective service in Chelyabinsk, and for the investment of his considerable expertise and influence in the idea. And I thank the Lord for Church of God Missionary Board President, Norm Patton, who listened to the prompting of the Holy Spirit, took a huge, courageous step of faith and pledged to send those 50 CoMission volunteers to Siberia.

An even more important figure in my personal part of the story is my wife, Vickie. Not only did she turn me loose for those two weeks in the spring of 1991, leaving her and our two small children home alone, but she gave permission to invest our entire family savings of $2,000 in the venture.

And of course, what would have happened if those six Florida high school students, Greg, Karis, Melanie, Sara, Shawn and Stephanie had not stepped forward and volunteered to go where no American had ever gone before.

Six ordinary teenagers, young, naïve, full of faith and perhaps some fears, willing to answer an unlikely call to travel to an unknown place to do whatever God had in store for them. No special qualifications, no impressive credentials, no outstanding abilities. Certainly no celebrity status. Just your everyday Jesus followers who obeyed God and helped change the world.

They are, and always will be, my heroes.

Epilogue

A Takeaway Challenge

Thank you for reading this book. Before you go, I have four lessons I learned from this experience that I would like to leave with you. I hope you will want to apply the first three to your walk with God, regardless of your age or season of life. If you are of high school age or a young adult, the final lesson is actually a personal challenge from me to you.

Lesson Number 1
Obedience is critical.
At the end of Chapter 14 of John, Jesus says, "The prince of this world is coming, but he has no hold on me. The world must learn that I love my Father so much that I will do exactly what my Father tells me to do" (*John 14:30-31*).

This is a remarkable statement by Jesus. He declares that Satan himself does not have a hold on Jesus and that Jesus' love for the Father is so great that He always does *exactly* what the Father tells him to do.

What a massive challenge for us as His followers! If we accept it, it means we will not allow the prince of this world to have a hold on us and we will always do exactly what the Father tells us to do. Is it possible, Jesus? How did you do this? These questions spin in my mind. But as always, God has not left us without an answer.

In the first eight verses of John 15, Jesus tells us how we too can live this life: "Remain in Him and He will remain in us, apart from Him we can do nothing." Take time to read these verses slowly.

"I am the true vine, and my Father is the gardener. He cuts off every branch in me that bears no fruit, while every branch that does bear fruit he prunes so that it will be even more fruitful. You are already clean because of the word I have spoken to you. Remain in me, as I also remain in you. No branch can bear fruit by itself; it must remain in the vine. Neither can you bear fruit unless you remain in me. I am the vine; you are the branches. If you remain in me and I in you, you will bear much fruit; apart from me you can do nothing. If you do not remain in me, you are like a branch that is thrown away and withers; such branches are picked up, thrown into the fire and burned. If you remain in me and my words remain in you, ask whatever you wish, and it will be done for you. This is to my Father's glory, that you bear much fruit, showing yourselves to be my disciples" (*John 15:1-8, NIV*).

Right there is the answer. We do *not* have to allow the prince of this world to have his hold on us, and we *can* live a life doing exactly what the Father tells us to do, *if* we make it a consistent practice to remain in Him.

This kind of lifestyle requires intentionality. Faithfulness in the small acts of obedience leads to greater opportunities of obedience. All of us must intentionally stay connected to the Vine, which is Jesus.

Lesson Number 2
Faith begets faith.

When we take simple steps of faith and say things like, "I'll go to Russia on this cultural exchange," we don't know the doors that will open for others as a result. If in that moment, Don Pickett and I would have turned down the possibility of going with David Stone to

Chelyabinsk, then the door could have closed permanently.

Being ready to respond to God's promptings not only impacts us, but others, as well. My wife visited Chelyabinsk in 1992. Three of my four children later spent time in Chelyabinsk. Some 50 CoMission volunteers lived in Chelyabinsk. A family of four spent almost a decade in this city. Russian pastors were raised up. Approximately 250 believers now worship in four churches there. Thousands of persons have been directly impacted at one level or another.

Our faith will always impact others. As I have said several times in this story, the opportunity of a lifetime is only available during the lifetime of the opportunity. If that be true, we should put ourselves in a position to listen closely to God's voice, and when He prompts, say, "Yes, Lord. Yes to your will and yes to your way."

Lesson Number 3
It's not about you.
Somebody once reminded me, "There is only one Messiah, and you are not Him."

You and I are part of something much bigger than ourselves. According to Ephesians 3:20, God's power is at work within us to accomplish immeasurably more than all we could ever ask or think. "God will take the foolish things in this world to confound the wise, so that no man will boast" (*I Corinthians 1:28-29*).

When seeking to position ourselves in a place where God can work through us, we sometimes think we are the center of the story. But don't forget, God does not choose the ones who will take all of the credit, but those who will give the glory to Him.

God chose me to lead the first student exchange, not because of who I was as a person. I just happened to be in the right place at the right time, willing and available for whatever He had in mind. For six years prior to November 1990, I was taking morning walks in the woods, praying that God would use me. In all honesty, my single greatest desire was to be a good pastor to the students I had been called to shepherd. I was not thinking at all about being part of God's activity in Russia. But He evidently had another plan.

Number 4
A final challenge to the next generation

I grew up in a broken home. I was not a popular student at school. I just sought to obey God's Word and trust Him with my future. That desire led me to Lake Wales, Florida, to prepare for whatever was next. In that place, God shaped me and formed me.

If you are one of those students who is not sure of what's coming next, but you have a heart for God and what He might want to do in your life, let me challenge you to take some time to take a close look at your future. I would dream for you the opportunity to complete a "gap year."

The year after you graduate high school or complete your undergraduate degree, wait on the Lord before launching into a college education, graduate work or a professional career. I believe that we serve a God who speaks. When you place yourself in a position to listen, you will hear His voice.

I do not believe that professional careers are either "sacred" or "secular." In 1 Peter 2:9 we read, "But you are a chosen people, a royal priesthood, a holy nation, God's special possession, that you may declare the praises of him who called you out of darkness into his wonderful light."

As a child of God, whatever God has wired you to do is sacred. Did God design you and call you to teach in public school? Then that is sacred work. Did He design and call you to work in retail sales? Then that is sacred. Did He call you to work full-time in the church? Then that is also sacred. Take a year and seek God's heart. Find out how He made you, and then step out and prepare yourself for what He wants to accomplish through you.

I suggest you use at least a portion of your gap year working with an organization specifically designed to help you discern God's direction for your life and career. Training programs offered by Youth with a Mission, Operation Mobilization, Teen Missions International, Heart to Honduras and other mission agencies are just a few among scores of opportunities. Be sure to check with your pastor about next-generation training programs in your own church or denomination.

While you are at it, I would challenge you to take a close look at two organizations close to my own heart that can help you prepare for whatever God has in store.

The H.E.A.R.T. Missionary Training Village, located in central Florida, has now been in operation for over 30 years. They have trained and equipped over one thousand students, and watched them go out to serve in more than 90 countries of the world.

A simulated Third World village, H.E.A.R.T. teaches small animal husbandry, sustainable agriculture, primary health care, appropriate technology, nutrition and food technology, cross-cultural communications, and community development. It was in the woods surrounding H.E.A.R.T. Village that I learned to wait on the Lord. Today, it still provides a setting where Jesus followers can seek God's heart for exactly what He wants them to do.

The Lake Wales Care Center is also located in central Florida. Its Care Corps comes alongside persons in the community and helps meet their basic needs. The heart of Care Corps is people helping people helping people. The Center provides family services, meals on wheels, transitional housing, a free clinic, a pregnancy care program to give expectant mothers choices, holiday assistance, literacy counseling and a community kitchen. It attracts volunteers who participate in stay-at-home mission camps, operate a youth coffee house, staff local thrift stores and provide many other community services.

Both H.E.A.R.T. Missionary Training Village and the Lake Wales Care Center offer semester-long study programs. Students spend 15 weeks in training, which includes an international experience to gain a global perspective. Some then become interns, working alongside a professional missionary. By then, many gap year veterans are ready to choose the trade school, college or advanced degree program that will prepare them for the career that God designed and called them to undertake.

God wants to use you at a level that you may not yet comprehend. He used me and He has plans for you! Don't settle for anything less. Make your life a challenge, not a compromise.

Appendix

Donald Pickett's private journal
Russian Exchange Trip
April 8-23, 1992

Outgoing
6:00 PM Left Lake Wales.
7:15 PM Arrived Days Inn.
5:50 AM Days Inn to Airport.
8:00 AM #1600 New York DELTA.
5:55 PM #102 Finnair to Helsinki. ARR 8:33 AM.
9:25 AM to Moscow. ARR 11:00 AM.
4:35 PM to Chelyabinsk. ARR 8:35 PM.

Day 1. April 8, 1992
To Orlando. Spent the entire day in the Executive
Council meeting. Things went well. Finally got away
from the office about 4 PM. Extremely tired, however
after resting and a few minutes packing got away about
6:55 PM. Arrived in Orlando, checked in at Days Inn.
Ed, Sheri, Jim Barringer, Earlene and I went to Ruby
Tuesdays for dinner. Got back to hotel about 9:30 PM.
Kareen and Ron arrived at 10 PM. Finally got to bed
about 11:15 PM.

April 9
Woke up about 3:50, couldn't go back to sleep. Finally
got up at 5:00. Left hotel at 5:50 to Airport. Everyone
was on time. Check-in went smoothly. Delta's agent
Debbie stayed with us until we boarded the plane.
Prayer circle before boarding. Parents and friends
waited until all were on. Plane left at 8 AM. Breakfast:
Melon, eggs, sausage, biscuit and milk. Arrived at New
York at 10:30 AM. Sylvia (Delta agent) met us and took

us to NY lounge. Relaxed until 2:15 PM. We left at 5:55 PM on 102 Finnair. Dave was late getting to NY. He brought our jackets. Meal on Finnair: Chicken, rice, mixed vegetables, pickled herring, tomatoes, chocolate. Believe it or not, I enjoyed the pickled herring. There was not much sleep; however, I did get a few winks. They woke us for breakfast 2½ hours later (short night). Breakfast was cheese croissant, salami croissant, melon. Beautiful flying over Norway and Sweden. The snow-capped mountains were beautiful. Helsinki was typical foreign city. Had to go outside to board plane for Moscow; 28 degrees that morning. Plane trip to Moscow was delightful. On landing in Moscow, we saw several sights from the air to indicate a very poor city. Houses in disrepair, lack of upkeep on most everything. We deplaned into a long, dark airport area through customs. No problem. Picked up our luggage and Dave spoke to agent. They did not check anything in any bag. Met by Tonya, Albert and Jim Albrecht. Jim had arrived a day early. Bus was waiting to take us into the city.

Boarded bus for ride into town. Very dirty city. Signs of underprivileged. Russian people are certainly in need. Long, long food lines. City buildings, government buildings all needed cleaning and upkeep. Amid all of this, the people were very gracious, kind, proud and loving. Drove through downtown Moscow—very different than our big cities. Less traffic for sure. Arrived at hotel for lunch. Lunch: Strips of pork, slaw, cucumbers and cream, noodle and mushroom soup, rice and hamburger croquet, carrots, warm Pepsi and ice cream. People wanted to sell almost everything (Caviar, Pepsi, etc.). Back on bus to airport (different). (Government) planes on apron of airport. Dirty, dingy, barn-like terminal. Checked luggage into holding area. Boarded plane. Heart sank! Plane unkempt, carpet torn, rolled up, dirty. Seat broken, plane packed, every seat taken. People wore heavy coats, put luggage on their laps. Did not obey "Fasten Seat Belt" signs. Took off for

Chelyabinsk. Certainly in God's Hands. Upon arrival in Chelyabinsk people met us with open arms. At airport, flowers, greetings, hugs, and we could feel the bond of love and friendship. On the plane, I met a man who spoke no English. I spoke no Russian. He saw my jacket "to Russia with God's Love." He began to go through his bag and pulled out a New Testament in Russian. Sign language was all that was spoken. Man in back of me tapped my shoulder. "Speak Russian?" "No." Dave and Tonya came. He wanted to know why I laughed and smiled. Dave told him it was because of God's love. A long conversation developed through Tonya, our interpreter. Man hungry for message of Christ. So appreciative! When we got off plane, I gave first man the Russian Bible Story Book by David C. Cook. He gripped my hand and shook it, on the plane and after when we got off the plane, did the same thing.

The Fields are White for the Harvest.

Upon arrival, we boarded a bus for the Rest Home. Traveled two hours. So tired upon arrival at Rest Home (typical C.O.G. Campground of '30s, except private rooms). Hot water. Again, welcomed with flowers, hot cake with salt. Assigned our rooms and dinner. It is now 12 midnight their time, 30 hours since we left Orlando. SO TIRED. Supper: Cukes/cream, Sliced pork/beef/chicken. Back to Dave's Room for party. Alexander and his teachers entertained the adults—vodka, caviar, pure chocolate, pickles. He presented each of us with a beautiful pocket watch with Ural Time. We toasted, toasted, toasted. Linda gave him the Proclamation for District Superintendent of Schools. Arlene gave a desk pen. Finally to bed 2:45 AM, Ural time.

April 10 (Earlene's Birthday)
We were able to sleep this A.M. Breakfast cukes, toast and cereal at noon. Following breakfast there was free time. The teachers of the school had brought some

beautiful jewelry. Ladies had a wonderful time. Bill, Ray, Ed and I walked out on the lake to see them ice fishing. Very entertaining. Lake was about 30 inches thick with ice. The fisherman had a small pole with a short line that reached below the surface of the ice. We just roamed the grounds. Ray gave two little children Frisbees. My, what joy! Father cried and could not thank us enough. Watched as children and youth tried old games of hopscotch. Lunch at 4 PM. Beef, fish, chicken slices, cukes, potato salad, soup, hamburger and beef, tea. After lunch, our group went back for a nap and rest. Thanks for the easy day. 8:00 PM supper. Beef, spam, fish, slice of cukes, beet salad, beef and macaroni, Japanese plums, tea. Mineral water at every meal. After supper we had a group meeting, sharing and rejoicing. The staff and management of the Rest Home had asked for a Bible study. Learned that State Education Rep. wanted to meet with us on Thursday the 16th. God is sure opening doors!

The Party. The teachers had learned today was Earlene's birthday. They prepared all day for her birthday party. One she will never forget. Tables set lovely. Squid, caviar, champagne, toasting, toasting, etc. Gifts you wouldn't believe! She is now a life-time teacher of School #31. Jewelry, stones. Tonya, Albert, Irena, Galena, Marsha, such beautiful ladies. Dancing, games, dancing, exchange of gifts. Party broke up at midnight. Glenna came to our room to express her love. Glenna and Earlene have become close friends. She is so precious. She gave Earlene 300 rubles (one week's pay). To bed at 1:30 AM. Oh Yes! The afternoon of today a Russian man came up to me and gave me a Russian Bible. Dave said "he wants conversation," so I got one of our Russian *Question and Answer Books about Life*. Saw him on a bench and spoke to him. Gave him the book. So appreciative! God help us to be your witnesses.

Saturday, April 11

Up at 7 AM (COLD). Breakfast today consisted of cakes, sausage, egg, rice, tea, toast and cheese. Left by bus for Chelyabinsk at nine-thirty. Arrived in town about 11:30 AM. Went to war memorial. Mother-daughter holding helmet; 20,000,000 Russians died in W.W.II. Every family touched. While at Memorial, a wedding party arrived. Russian custom for bride and groom to take flowers to many memorials on wedding day. Ray and Randy decided to give gifts. Ray not a stranger to anyone. The party wanted to toast Ray so they brought out 8 oz. glasses. It turned out to be a very humorous experience. On to memorial of Russian who was the father of the nuclear program in Russia. Chelyabinsk is an industrial city only open to America a year ago. Went to museum. From museum to School #31. Students are receptive. Every teacher wanted us to see their classroom. Randy, Arlene, Linda in Seventh Heaven. Visited Albert's room (Russian Literature), English Room, Computer Room, then to cafeteria for lunch. Appetizer: raisins, slaw, dried apricots, dried berries (like cranberries). Soup: egg. Main: fried pork, potatoes, and beets. Dessert: cake. Drink: apple juice, mixed fruit juices. They boil several kinds of fruits and add sugar.

Earlene talked to food service manager concerning food service. He gave her his knife, bottle opener from his key ring. Most Giving People! On leaving the school, we went to the Sports Complex and Pioneer Museum (like our YMCA). Arts and sports are taught here. The U.S. kids go home and watch TV. Russian children go to dancing, martial arts, painting, rock collecting, etc. Russian people are very "arts minded." Two hours back to Rest Home. Time for supper: Cukes, beets, sausage, bread, etc. Relaxed rest of evening. Went to bed at 10:45 PM, awakened at 12:00, invited to party on second floor.

THOUGHTS

>> Russians are certainly more culture-minded than Americans.

>> Russian People are generous, kind, loving, friendly, and very lovely people

>> They must get to know you before warming up to you.

>> So far I have noticed much talk about the government.

>> Salaries are low! Teacher receive 1,000 rubles a month (American $10.00)

>> They are very proud but poor people.

>> Alexander remarked, "Don't give us food, money, or material things. Give us teachers and help us in education. Help us to teach each other. Education is the important thing."

Sunday, April 12

Got up at 8:30 AM. Good night's rest. Cold today. Breakfast was served at 10 this morning. Cukes, hamburger, potatoes, cheese, toast and cookies. After breakfast we met in the hall for a great service! Ed spoke, Cheri and Arlene did music. New Way group sang, testimonies. Russian teachers and students gave wonderful witness. It snowed today. The kids really had a marvelous time together. Snow balls flew! Lunch--it seems we eat all the time--was cuke/radish salad, rice and beef soup, hamburger, tea. Meals are good. After lunch, Jim, Mark, Dave, Ed, Ray and I meet with a Russian evangelist concerning the work in Russia. Seems we decided on a crusade in 1993 in Chelyabinsk. There is some talk of Mark coming as a missionary. Relaxed the rest of afternoon and evening. Kids enjoyed Russian bath house. Supper at 7 PM. Noodles with liver, potatoes, cuke salad, crepes, tea. Following supper, all adults went to bath house. Quite an experience. You go into the sauna, get up a good sweat, cold shower, pool (cold), you repeat this three times. During the first sauna experience, you are beaten with tree branches. The whole experience sure makes you feel good.

Monday, April 13
Breakfast at 8:30 AM. Boarded bus at 9 AM to Chelyabinsk, 2 hours. It is sure a long time. Chelyabinsk is 77 miles from where we stay. 11:40 met with the mayor, the commission of economy and the education commission. The mayor spoke for many minutes explaining their city. Industry is the primary work. Mark introduced us. I present American flag. Mark gave presentation from Lake Wales and Vero Beach. Earlene gave gifts to all council people. We left City Hall to go to the Organ Hall. WOW! What a concert! 1½ hours of organ, cello and a splendid choir.
From the concert to the school. Lunch: fruit, vegetables, juice, soup, meat, potatoes, cake. We collected $785 to change into rubles.

From the school to the post office. Left the post office for the Rest Home. 2 Hours. It sure makes you tired. Arrived back about 8:20 PM. Supper: potato salad, meat slices, stew and cookies. Everyone was so tired that about 9:30 the gang started going to bed. Retired at 10:30.

Tuesday, April 14
Breakfast 10 AM. Cukes, ham slices, liver, potatoes, egg soufflé. After breakfast, we went to the hall to hear and sing Russian songs. A lot of fun! There were small group meetings among our small groups. Lunch at 3 PM. Meat slices (beef, turkey, smoked salmon) noodle soup, beef and mashed potatoes, tomatoes with garlic and horseradish. Interesting dessert of cottage cheese/raisins and sugar. Following the lunch time, a group met with some of the Russian maids for Bible

study). They wanted another one, so Saturday AM was set.

[**Insert:** Monday evening I had a good conversation with Ed concerning our state work. I shared some concerns and he was of the opinion I should share my feelings with the personnel committee.]

Continuation of April 14

Supper on Tuesday consisted of beef and noodles, tea, salmon, and turkey strips. Following supper, we went to the great hall and sang many Russian songs, some American songs and then more Russian. They had planned a party for the adults: cookies, candy, lemonade, vodka, and there was much toasting. We finally got to bed about 1:00 AM.

Wednesday, April 15

Got up about 8:00 AM. Breakfast at 9:00 AM. Fried eggs, potatoes, meat slices, butter, smoked salmon, tea. Boarded bus at 10:10 for town. Arrived about 12:30 at Drama Theater. Distributed money to kids. Met our guest family, Mikhail, an exporter of food and clothing, his wife a doctor (cardiologist). She was not practicing but raising her family. Two children, Mary Ann, 7 yrs., and George, 4. Both beautiful children. We went to the market place (a mall in the United States), one-building-with-everything. Then to the food market, comparable to a flea market in America. No refrigeration. Meat cut many ways, just hung out on the counter. Russia is a very impoverished country. People have no faith in government.

Back to their home, a small flat, probably no more than 32 x 15 feet, four rooms and bath. A delicious meal: sour cukes, tomatoes, deviled eggs with caviar, vegetable salad. Crab, calzones, sardines, potato, apple, pork, champagne, apricot juice, what we would call BBQ pork, black plums, carrots, Russian ice cream, nuts and tea. Earlene had coffee with ice cream in it. Visited with family and two girls (Mary Ann and Lula). Following dinner we went to the theater to see drama "Bliss." Mick and Onan took us. We met the rest of the group. "Bliss" was a story of a lover with four lovers. One wanted him to marry another and get her money and then he would leave her and come to the first love. Quite complicated. Last act all were very scantily dressed. I think it must have embarrassed our hosts.

After drama, back to home. Another meal of sausage, pickles and cheese sandwiches, salad and tea. Talked with family for a long while concerning traditions and feelings. Basic, Government is corrupt. They don't trust leadership. Feel they will come out of economy/depression. Went to bed about 11 PM.

(*Note*) Mick's mother called. He said she calls several times a day to see how he is. (Mothers the same in every land)

Thursday, April 16, 1992

Got up about 7:45 to be at school by 9:00 AM. We had a nice breakfast. Tossed salad, pork salad, juice, tea, toast with egg and caviar. We arrived at the school by 9 AM. First grade program, then to the sixth grade English lesson. Children very knowledgeable about English. Every child in the school (1000) must take English. Mick picked us up at 12:30. Visited several shops. Earlene bought jewelry at a shop that required a ticket. Jewelry very expensive according to rubles. Following shopping, we went to pick up Onan's English Teacher, Nellie. Nellie was overjoyed to meet Americans. She talked and talked. We went to lunch at the Business Men's Lounge. Very unusual. Checked coats, went down a steep flight of stairs (like a boat or ship stairs) into a beautiful room: hardwood floors, tables all set. Menu: Liverwurst, 3lb. pieces, tongue, cheese, egg, Russian pastries, Pepsi (warm), salad of cukes, tomatoes and onions, steak (10 oz.), potatoes, radishes, Jell-O, cranberries.

After dinner, back to school for performances. Russian play (serious) I did not understand. (Something about animals in forest). Back to family and rested for an hour. Then to the Russian Ballet: *Nutcracker Suite.* Very beautiful. Building was breathtaking with all this gold. The ballet lasted about 2 hours. Dancing very, very beautiful. Back to home for supper at 9:30 PM. Dumplings with cheese and mushrooms, bread and butter, sour tomatoes. They insisted we try their Russian-Jewish tradition of vodka with sour tomatoes and cukes. Tomato killed the taste some. Could only swallow. Talked about Russian-Jewish traditions and history. Some of their ancestors had fled to the Urals away from Hitler. Gave them gifts from Freedlander for Russian-Jewish mother. I had eaten so much. Fruit, prunes, apricot juice. My stomach was not feeling the best. To bed at 12:00 midnight. It was an educational day and a wonderful opportunity.

Friday, April 17

Forgot to mention yesterday our visit to the open market, Russian Orthodox Church Mass. Got up this morning about 8:30 AM. For breakfast had fish, cukes, tomatoes, pickled peppers, tea, ice cream with nuts, sliced pork, and bread. They are such a fine family. George was full of life this morning. We left to meet the bus around 10:25. The kids were real excited about their home stays. Many, many gifts were given. The mayor brought his sons to go with us back to the base. Christianity and Americanism are sure making inroads. Tears were shed as the bus pulled out. Max brought us more gifts. Tonya, Luba, Galena, Albert all came with us on the bus. They took us to a jewelry store. It was so small the group spent almost two hours. Then through new development of the city. Many, many flats being built.

Got back to the base about 5 PM. Supper ready. Man, do we eat! Rice, beef, soup, bread and tea. Following supper, we had two hours of Russian folk songs and games. Jim, Ed, Mark and I tried to get together some proposals for the (Education) Commission. They are extremely hungry for education, Bible and English. Mark and Jim met with him (Mayor of Education) at 9 PM. They accepted our proposals; now for them to be approved by the Missionary Board and the city government. 10 PM: Another big party. Wine, caviar, beef, bread. Toasting, toasting and more gifts. They brought an artist who painted our portraits. Russian ice cream (sure is good) and the expensive chocolate. To bed about 1:30 AM. Mark Boyer cut his finger about one o'clock, so the doctor had to put stitches in it.

Saturday, April 18
Breakfast at 9:00: Cukes and radishes, liver, potatoes, bread and tea. Following the breakfast, we had a worship service for any who wanted to come. Over 115 people showed up. Ed chaired, I prayed, Jim spoke, Ray sang "He's Got the Whole World." My, people are hungry. Communism certainly destroyed all they had-- self-worth, hope, joy and peace. They cried, they hugged, so appreciative.

Left then to go to the mineral museum. Most outstanding. I looked at a desk set; Alexandria bought it for me. Such giving people. We came back and then went to the woods (forest) for a picnic. Flavored mineral water, one-half chicken boiled, tongue, beef, eggs, cukes, pickles, bread. Interesting the reaction of the kids to tongue. Earlene and Cheri came back early. Ed was sick, Earlene had a headache. The kids sang, played games and had a delightful time. Got back to the room about 5:45 PM. Tired!! After a nap, supper was at 7:00 PM. Cukes, crepes, beef and noodles, tea. After supper, Ed, Mark, Jim and I went to discuss Sunday's activities. Kids are extremely tired and some are sick. So we decided to make some changes.

Schedule for Sunday.
9:00 Breakfast.
10:00 Worship. Song and Prayer, Mark to speak on commitment, then Ed, followed by Communion with Don.
2:00 Ed and Jim to meet with new converts. Don and Mark to meet with Florida delegates.
3:00 Lunch.
4:00-5:00 Packing.
5:00 Baptismal.
6:00-9:00 Going Away Party.
9:00 Kids to Bed
10:00 Adults to Bed
2:45 Rise and Shine

After our meeting, I came back to the room. Earlene was sacked out. Many adults went to the bath house. I went to bed at 10:30. (During the evening, they brought ice cream, and gifts. They don't seem to be able to give enough).

Sunday – Easter, April 19, 1992
Up at 7:00 AM. Good night's sleep!!! Breakfast at 9:00. Earlene in bed with a headache. At breakfast: cukes, liver/rice, tea, cheese curds/raisins/sugar. Needless to say I had tea with bread. Easter service at 10:00 AM. Ed played on the guitar some pre-service music as people gathered. The place filled up. We sang some songs, "Father I Adore You," "Jesus Loves Me." Ed prayed and then Mark spoke. A very simple message on love, resurrection and what it means to be a Christian. Ed then gave a very simple invitation. Four steps in salvation: Confession, repentance, belief, acceptance. He had all of us come to the front who were already

Christians. Then a simple prayer of salvation. He then asked those who had prayed the prayer and had accepted Christ and who would live for Him to come forward. Thirty-three people came. Ray almost shouted. The Spirit of God was so real. What rejoicing. They were so hungry. Several from the village accepted Him.

Then I was to lead communion. Wow! what an experience. I had bread from the kitchen which was filling. The juice was plum juice. They brought it to me in a big soup tureen instead of a little bowl. I had them come and break the bread and dip it in the juice. I gave the story of Jesus's last meal with the disciples, read the scripture and prayed. Students and teachers came forward with counterparts. What rejoicing. Tears flowed. The artist who accepted Christ came, greeted me, hugged me and just wept. What an experience. As I write, my soul is thrilled. It was one of the best Easter services I had ever experienced!!

After the service we had some free time. At 2:00, Ed and Jim met with the new converts for instruction. Mark and I met with the Florida delegation. Lunch at 3:00. Same type of food. Getting a little tired. After lunch the departure activities began. Games, testimonies and tears. 5:00 PM supper. Packing after supper. Earlene up and around now. Irena and Mikhail drove out from Chelyabinsk to see us. They had read the Bible story book. Had many questions. Why did Jesus have to die? What does Christianity believe? How many Christians in America? We talked for quite a while. They are hungry. They brought gifts for us. Kitchen set for Earlene. Tie bar for me. The music teacher came with them. We gave her granddaughter and Maryanne the Barbie dolls. What rejoicing. George got football cards. They left about 4:30 PM.

After supper we had a baptismal service at the Bath House. Nineteen followed the Lord in baptism. Many from the village. Luka, Galena, Tonya, Albert and several of the kids. Another time of rejoicing. Following the Baptismal service, the adults had a party. Words of appreciation, rejoicing and tears. To bed at 11:00 PM. Tired, exhausted (mentally and physically) but HAPPY!!

Monday, April 20
Up at 2:00 AM, loaded bus and left at 3 AM. Just before leaving, a young girl baptized the night before came to me as I was loading the bus. She handed me her big, well-used and loved stuffed monkey, along with a ruble on which she had written her name and address. It is worn, dirty, loved and big. It was the best she had. I came unglued!! I would much rather have refused and given it back, but I would have hurt her in that way. I don't know when anything moved me as much. It will go in my office as a constant reminder of God's great gift of Jesus Christ to me!!

A police escort to the airport, 77 miles. The mayor and Commissioner of Education had sent it. Man, we made it to town in record time! You would think we were celebrities. Our plane left at 7:25 AM. Goodbyes at the airport were hard. Arrived in Moscow at 7:25 AM. Two hours difference in time. What a day they had planned for us. From the airport to hotel for breakfast; crepes, eggs, bread, butter and tea. Earlene is sure hungry for coffee. Dave Stone stayed long enough to meet us before he and Jim left.

Next, a three-hour tour of Moscow: a great Orthodox Church, downtown Moscow. Earlene and I commented throughout the day that we had to pinch ourselves to make sure we really realized what was happening. Moscow is a very beautiful city. First impressions at the airport were deceiving. Good roads, wide streets. We spent 1 hour inside the Kremlin. What a beautiful building. Gold, cleanliness, etc. Commercialism quite prevalent. Hucksters on the outside wanted to sell everything. Capitalism is prevalent. Bartering on the streets was quite a sight. Thousands with their wares. Saw the tomb of the Unknown Soldier, Eternal Flame.

We did not get to visit Red Square. We saw it, but could not enter. Congress in session and there had been demonstrations for Communism.

Back to hotel and checked in at Sputnik Hotel. Interesting, to say the least. Bathroom with shower, two cots, TV. To Sports Hotel for lunch. Pork, mixed veggies, soup, beet and cabbage salad, ice cream, and orange pop. Back to hotel to rest. Had only one hour. Showered and prepared for evening. At 4:30, we went to change money, which took about one and a half hours. Then to McDonalds for supper. Arrived too late to eat supper so we went to the opera. We all were so tired and hungry that we left during intermission. Back to McDonalds. I have never enjoyed a cheeseburger so much in my life! This is the World's Largest McDonald's, one city block long! They have had to close the street in front and put up guides for the lines. Each day they are lined several city blocks for the good old American Hamburger! Back to Hotel. To bed at 10. Totally exhausted!

Tuesday, April 21
Up at 7:00 AM. Raining today and cold. The bus that was to take us to breakfast was late coming. Finally, at 9:30 we boarded a city bus and went to the Sports Hotel. What an experience. People push and shove. "Get out of my way," seems to be the general attitude. Ed had his pocket picked. They got $20. Our bus came while we were at breakfast. After breakfast, to the Art Museum. They would not let me in with my passport case, so I did not get to see the museum. I went back to the bus and slept. At 1:30 we went back to Sports Hotel for lunch. Creamed gizzards, noodle, cukes and tea, and ice cream. To Arbat Street to shop. Quite interesting. A lot of bartering. We got one tea pot, "Samovar." Then to Pizza Hut for supper. Good ole American food. Salad was $4.00. Large pizzas were $19.00. Then to the Circus. WOW!! A Russian circus is a real adventure. Tamed birds, bears, camels, and

many, many more acts. Circus lasted about 3 hours but was an experience you would not want to miss. To bed around 11:30 PM.

Wednesday, April 22
Breakfast at Sport Hotel. Then off to the Russian Orthodox Church. It was cold, snowing, wind blowing. Hats and gloves were welcomed. Mark had told us just a jacket. The kids were ready to shoot him. The Orthodox religion is very formal and ritualistic; so much so, it is no wonder people are so hungry for the gospel. Back to Moscow. The weather is terrible. Twenty-one went to the ballet. The rest of us stayed and rested, packed and visited.
The group returned about eleven. We then had a birthday party for Tonya. To bed at 12 midnight.

Thursday, April 23, 1992
Homeward Bound. Up at 6 AM Russian time (10 PM American time). Checked out of the hotel at 8:00 AM and left for Sports Hotel for breakfast. Visited the Metro station (such beautiful mosaic tiles on the walls), then to Red Square. Group pictures and visit to Lenin's tomb. To the Airport. Lined up as suggested. Went right through customs with no bag search. Boarded plane (Finnair to Helsinki). On the plane, we met the niece of Don and Bobby Sims. Arrived in Helsinki on time and had 30 minutes to board plane for New York. Seven hours 40 minutes to New York. Two meals and a lot of memories shared. Arrived in New York at 3:50 PM. Went right through customs and transferred to Delta terminal. Had about 30 minutes after the gang arrived at Delta. Boarded plane to Orlando, one hour late leaving due to computers being down. We had now been up 26 hours. Finally left and arrived in Orlando at 9:15 PM. Our entire group stayed on the plane until everyone else was off. We de-boarded singing "Lord, I Adore You." My, what a welcome! Balloons, posters, cheers, and

kisses and hugs. Had a group picture taken. Finally got away from airport after 10:00 PM. Keith, Delyn and Karen met us. Keith had not eaten, so all of us went to Denny's. Home at 12 midnight. Thirty-two hours without sleep. Our bed looked so good after our baths and reading some of the mail. Great experience!
Thank you Lord!!

Index of Names

Second Cultural Exchange/Missions Team
April 1992
(Listed by day of the week each committed to pray and fast for the trip's success.)

Sunday
Amanda Powderly (Pembroke Pines, Florida)
Chris Mazzarella (Vero Beach, Florida)
Dawn Womack (Vero Beach, Florida)
Ginny Walsh (Sebastian, Florida)
Monica Piper (Lake Wales, Florida)

Monday
Megan Newberry (Lake Wales, Florida)
Michele Drusell (Vero Beach, Florida)
Ray Roberts (Lake Wales, Florida)
Sarah Johnson (Jacksonville, Florida)
Stacy Wilbraham (Clearwater, Florida)

Tuesday
Jim Albrecht (Cairo, Egypt)
Karis Blunden (Bradenton, Florida)
Kelli Brooks (Vero Beach, Florida)
Marc Boyer (Sarasota, Florida)

Wednesday
Erik Warm (Orlando, Florida)
Jason Cole (Clearwater, Florida)
Mark Simon (Vero Beach, Florida)
Robert McGarvey (Vero Beach, Florida)

Thursday
Don Pickett (Lake Wales, Florida)
Earlene Pickett (Lake Wales, Florida)
Heather Wolford (Plant City, Florida)
Margie Gollehur (Interlachen, Florida)
Ron Beard (Lake Wales, Florida)

Friday
Cheri Nelson (Lake Wales, Florida)
Ed Nelson (Lake Wales, Florida)
Linda Fasel (Lake Wales, Florida)
Mark Shaner (Vero Beach, Florida)
Vickie Shaner (Vero Beach, Florida)

Saturday
Arlene Portwood (Lake Wales, Florida)
Greg Campbell (Lake Wales, Florida)
Randy Portwood (Lake Wales, Florida)
Bill Barringer (Lake Wales, Florida)
James Barringer (Lake Wales, Florida)

Third Cultural Exchange/Missions Team
August 1993
(Hometown information unavailable. Listed by prayer and fasting schedule.)

Sunday
Terry Fasel
Gary Howell
Lynda Neger
Kerri Mitchell

Monday
Stephanie Muhlenforth
Ellen Jerrils

Kareen Pickett
Bruce Seger

Tuesday
Michael Barber
Ron Beard
Avalynda Casey
Steve Casey
Mark Shaner

Wednesday
Bernie Joyner
Ben Fink
Amanda Fosson
Greg Sempsrott

Thursday
Jason Cole
Greg McCaw
Lori McCaw
Dennis Mitchell
Etta Mae Mitchell

Friday
Jennifer Pierce
Ken Long
Mavis Presson
Ron Wilcox

Saturday
Zoe McKenzie
Diana Poland
Joan Dixon
Ken Sifford

CoMission Volunteers

(Sent by the Missionary Board of the Church of God between 1994 and 1998 for one-year assignments as Special Assignment Missionaries.)

Mark Berg
Winnipeg, Manitoba

Cindy Binkerd
(Mauritson)
Olympia, Washington

William Bridgeman
Cindy Bridgeman
Davison, Michigan

Connie Callos
Vancouver, Washington

Kay Clark
Columbia City, Indiana

Eileen Clay
Anderson, Indiana

Calvin Brallier
Martha Brallier
Frankfort, Indiana

Tricia Bullock
Lake Wales, Florida

Thomas Cockerham
Janet Cockerham
Lexington, Kentucky

Annie Friedrich
Flint, Michigan

Dwayne Goldman
Kara Goldman
Lake Wales, Florida

Chris Groeber
Jeannette Groeber
Mount Sterling,
Kentucky

Johnathan Hart
Mary Hart
Murfreesboro,
Tennessee

Freda Jordan
(Hamilton)
Clackamas, Oregon

Orlo Kretlow
Carol Kretlow
Vancouver, Washington

Julie Lund
North Bergen, New
Jersey

Carol Naugher
(VanDerHeyden)
Wilmore, Kentucky

Amber Otis
Hillsboro, Ohio

Charles Sandlin
Bernell Sandlin
Claremore, Oklahoma

Angela Rhodes
Acworth, Georgia

Ruthann Tefft
Holland, Michigan

Elroy Weixel
Harriet Weixel
Jerome, Idaho

Joel Workman
Denver, Colorado

(Author's note: The above list appears to be incomplete, perhaps due to the destruction of some Missionary Board archives when the agency was dissolved and its offices moved to new facilities at Church of God Ministries, Inc. If you or someone you know served as a CoMission volunteer and your name does not appear here, please accept our apology. Contact davidlmiller10@gmail.com to correct the omission in future editions of this book. Thank you.)

Published sources consulted for this book

Books

Eshleman, Paul with Carolyn E. Phillips. *I Just Saw Jesus: The JESUS Film – From vision, to reality, to the unimaginable.* Aneko Press.

Johnson, Cheryl Barton and Donald D. Johnson, with Lester A. Crose. *Into All the World: A century of Church of God Missions.* Anderson, IN: Warner Press, 2009.

Johnson, Paul H., ed. with Bruce Wilkinson. *The CoMission: The amazing story of eighty ministry groups working together to take the message of Christ's love to the Russian people.* Chicago: Moody Publishers, 2004.

Periodicals and Digital Media

Baurain, Bradley. CoMission and Alliance see gains in former U.S.S.R. *World Pulse*, 7 January 1994: 4-5.

Chelyabinsk, n.d. *Wikipedia, the free encyclopedia.* Retrieved December 31, 2013 from https://en. wikipedia.org/wiki/Chelyabinsk

Church of God Missions, Dondeena Caldwell, editor. Anderson, IN: Missionary Board of the Church of God. June 1993, March/April 1996.

Cold War, n.d. *Wikipedia, the free encyclopedia.* Retrieved December 30, 2013 from https://en. wikipedia.org/wiki/Cold_War

Cornell, George W. Coached by Americans, Ex-Soviet Schools Teaching Christian Ethics (Associated Press). *The Press Journal*, Indian River County, Florida, 26 June 1993.

Dilalla, Patricia. From Russia, With Love: Group arrives from Vero Beach's Sister City. *The Press Journal*, Indian River County, Florida, 20 November 1992: A-1.

Fasel, Linda. Lake Waleans in Group Visit Russia. *The Lake Wales News*, 28 May 1992: 6.

_____ To Russia with God's Love. *Church of God News*, June 1992.

Glasnost, n.d. *Wikipedia, the free encyclopedia.* Retrieved December 30, 2013 from https://en. wikipedia.org/wiki/Glasnost

Lunkin, Roman. Traditional Pentecostals in Russia. *East-West Church and Ministry Report*, Vol. 12, No. 3, Summer 2004. Retrieved from http://www. eastwestreport.org/articles/ew12302.html

Mikhail Gorbachev, n.d. *Wikipedia, the free encyclopedia.* Retrieved December 30, 2013 from https://en.wikipedia.org/wiki/Mikhail_Gorbachev

Miller, David. Abre Puerta a Rusia: Un equipo de educadores cristianos se prepara para iniciar instrucciones de la Biblia en las escuelas públicas de Chelyabinsk. *La Trompeta*, noviembre/diciembre de 1993: 12-13.

_____ Protecting Russia from Evangelical Influences: A conversation with Alexander Sorokin. *Compass Direct News*, 22 November 1996: 16-17.

Pera, Eric. Students' Trip made religious impact on Russian residents. *The Ledger*, Lakeland, Florida, 1992

Perestroika, n.d. *Wikipedia, the free encyclopedia.* Retrieved December 30, 2013 from https://en. wikipedia.org/wiki/Perestroika

Russian Orthodox , n.d. *Wikipedia, the free encyclopedia.* Retrieved December 30, 2013 from https: //en.wikipedia.org/wiki/Russian_Orthodox_Church

Thomas, Cal. The Bible: Welcome in Russia, discarded by American society. Los Angeles Times Syndicate, *Los Angeles Times,* 17 April 1992.

Union of Evangelical Christians-Baptists of Russia, n.d. *Wikipedia, the free encyclopedia.* Retrieved April 10, 2014 from https://en.wikipedia.org/wiki/Union_of_ Evangelical_Christians-Baptists_of_Russia

CPSIA information can be obtained
at www.ICGtesting.com
Printed in the USA
FSHW020147110120
65769FS